101
Games and Activities
for Canoes and Kayaks

Diane Tyrrell

ISBN: 978-1-60679-155-4
Library of Congress Control Number: 2011920667
Cover design: Brenden Murphy
Book layout: Studio J Art & Design
Section pages illustration: Dynamic Graphics
Front cover photo: Comstock Images

Healthy Learning
P.O. Box 1828
Monterey, CA 93942
www.healthylearning.com

Limitations and Disclaimer of Liability

The games and activities in this book are intended to be used to complement and reinforce skills as part of a paddling instructional curriculum that is taught and supervised by qualified individuals. Those instructors using this material are expected to have the ability, knowledge, and skills to teach and supervise boating activities, as applicable to the types of boats, waterways utilized, and clienteles served.

It is the responsibility of the people using the material in this book to ensure that activities are conducted in a safe manner, with an understanding that the instruction and supervision of boating activities demands a professional level of competency, and that those instructors conducting activities demonstrate personal responsibility and an ability to promote safety in a potentially hazardous activity.

The games and activities in this book are intended for use on flatwater, and whitewater only up to Class III difficulty, as defined by the American Version of the International Scale of River Difficulty, and that any whitewater activities are conducted only on water that has been run and rated.

Any practices, guidelines, policies, procedures, or recommendations described herein are not associated or affiliated with any voluntary or mandatory accreditation or certification program, and no attempt is made to encompass every possible practice that may be desirable. Compliance with and/or the use of anything described, written or implied, within *101 Games and Activities for Canoes and Kayaks* does not guarantee that a boating activity will be safe, or that participants will be free from harm. The expectation is that those instructors utilizing this material have the responsibility for understanding and implementing responsible risk management practices.

All participants, and those individuals and programs offering paddlesports activities, must understand that swimming and boating, including in an outdoor or wilderness setting, includes inherent and other risks, hazards, and dangers that can cause injury, damage, disability, paralysis, death, or other loss, and that these risks and dangers may be caused by their own actions or inactions, or the actions or inactions of others participating in the activity, In choosing to voluntarily engage in paddlesports, participants must understand that they assume the inherent risks of these activities, and share in the responsibility for their own well-being, including to discontinue participation if they believe conditions to be unsafe.

Diane Tyrrell, contributing writers, and any current or future related individuals or entities, disclaim all duty, responsibility, or liability to organizations, participants, users, or any other individuals or entities for any injury, death, or other loss resulting from any cause, including but not limited to injury, death, or other loss, claimed to be caused, in whole or in part, by an organization's or individual's use of or adherence to the information or practices included in *101 Games and Activities for Canoes and Kayaks*, written or implied (or those contained in any future or related editions).

Dedication

This book is dedicated to my parents, with a thank you for sending me to summer camp for the very first time. And to my Pap, for giving me the courage to jump out of the boat, and always pulling me back in when I did.

Acknowledgments

The games and activities in *101 Games and Activities for Canoes and Kayaks* are derived from many sources. Many of the games and activities are of my original creation, some are adaptations of traditional games, some are combinations of ideas, and some have been learned along the way as I built my teaching toolbox.

As sharing is the typical nature of those who enthusiastically teach outdoor recreational activities, some of the games and activities in this book have been passed down and modified from many generations of paddlers and instructors, and I would like to thank the myriad youth leaders, camp counselors, and instructors for sharing their love of paddlesports.

It is possible that those people who passed along some of the games and activities included in this book found their information in material that may have appeared in another publication. Best efforts have been made to reference the sources for the games and activities presented in this publication. Those readers who are aware of any reference for which this book has failed to adequately provide the proper credit, please let the publisher know so that this information can be included in any future editions.

Many thanks go out to those who have been my instructors, mentors, and friends over these many years. Specific thanks to Randy Drake, Paul Greggs, Greg Cronin, Cathy Scheder, my camp counselors at Camp Tweedale (with an extra shout-out to Evie "Baby J Bear," for letting me live past the age of 10), and a special thanks to my son David, for inventing the Vampire Tag game.

Thanks also to all of my camp friends, paddling buddies, staff, and volunteers, who I have had the pleasure to paddle with. Additionally, I would like to express my appreciation to the many camp staff who have worked with me for always teaching me something, too. I would also like to thank and acknowledge my professional camping colleagues, as well as the staff and volunteers with the American Camp Association. Great appreciation also goes out to the myriad volunteers and staff with the American Red Cross and American Canoe Association for all of your dedication to paddlesports training.

A very special thank you goes to my husband for a zillion hours of proofreading and several missed meals in putting this book together, and to my sons for always being a playful inspiration.

Contents

PART 1

GETTING READY TO PLAY

1

Supervision and Safety

Photo Courtesy of The U.S. Coast Guard

Prior to Playing: Supervision

Risks are inherent in all aquatics and paddlesports activities—even if you are simply having fun playing games in canoes and kayaks. Anytime people are participating in paddlesports, the chance that someone will fall in, capsize, or have a medical emergency in or near the water increases. Safety at all times while on and around the water should be top priority, and the people supervising boating activities must be diligent in protecting participants against risk of injury.

A critical safety factor is to ensure that the people supervising boating activities are well-trained. Nothing takes the place of high-quality instruction and supervision. The games and activities in this book are intended to be used in conjunction with paddling instructional curriculum, taught and supervised by qualified individuals. The people supervising and instructing boating activities set the examples—in both attitudes and actions—which directly impact participant safety.

Ideally, the people supervising boating games and activities should, at minimum, have:

- Teaching ability, preferably with an instructor certification from a nationally recognized boating organization, specific to the type(s) of craft and bodies of water to be used
- Competent paddling ability, specific to the type(s) of craft and bodies of water to be used
- Knowledge, paddling ability, and skills required to execute rescue in a quick and effective manner in an emergency, specific to the type(s) of craft and bodies of water to be used
- Excellent judgment and mature decision-making
- Physical fitness and physical ability to execute emergency skills/rescue
- Knowledge of emergency action plans, and the ability to effectively implement the plans
- Knowledge of the waterway(s) to be used, including ability to recognize and respond to hazards
- Ability to relate in a positive manner with the clientele served
- Compliance with all standards, regulations, and laws as applicable

It is also highly recommended that an adult with certification/training in CPR and first aid from a nationally recognized organization be present and easily accessible. For boating activities that take place where access by, or contact with, emergency medical services is limited, or when access to professional medical help would take more than one hour, an adult who has additional CPR and first aid certification from a nationally recognized organization in wilderness-level first aid (or higher) should be present.

It's easy to underestimate the fitness, finesse, and technical skills required to be a good paddler. Like most sports, paddling is not a skill that a person learns and masters to the level of being able to teach, supervise, or effectively execute rescue in a one- or two-day learn-to-paddle course. Ideally, the people supervising boating activities should be experienced paddlers, specifically in the type(s) of boats and on the types of water used in the program. This aspect is critical to safety, as an experienced paddler will generally have better boat control and ability to execute rescue in a quick and efficient manner than someone who has just started paddling. An experienced boater is also more likely to have skills in his own paddling repertoire to keep participants motivated for learning, meeting their needs for progression as well.

Program operators should consider requiring a skills verification of the people who are instructing and supervising boating activities. Skills verification helps ensure that the people supervising boating activities have the paddling ability and knowledge to conduct activities, as well as the physical ability to perform the skills required.

Please note that these qualifications are the suggested minimum for the people supervising activities. Operators should evaluate the supervision needs of their boating program specific to the facilities, body of water, boats used, activities conducted, and clientele served. Some organizations—such as camps and agencies serving youth groups—have specific standards for the supervision of boating activities. Additionally, local, state, or federal laws and regulations may dictate how activities must be conducted and supervised. People supervising boating activities should be familiar with the standards and regulations applicable to the program, facility, and body of water, and conduct activities in compliance.

As a matter of "better practices" in conducting activities safely, program operators may also want to consider some additional program requirements:
- Minimum supervisor/instructor-to-participant ratios
- Requirements for how many supervisors/instructors must be adults
- Written requirements for the conduct of people supervising boating activities
- Requirements for the verification of skills of those supervising boating activities

Prior to Playing: Location of Supervisors/Instructors

During all on-water games and activities, supervisors should be positioned:
- In close proximity to participants, in order to readily assist and quickly execute rescue
- Where they can easily see all of the participants and quickly account for everyone

The people who have a responsibility to execute rescue for boating activities should "be where the action is," positioned on the water, close to participants. For some activities, supervisors should be stationed where they are set up and prepared for rescue, such as standing at the ready with a throw bag when participants are running a rapid.

A Note About the Use of Lifeguards in Supervising Boating Games and Activities

While the use of a lifeguard in the supervision of boating activities may be well-intended, unless the lifeguard has competent paddling ability, boat control skills, and the knowledge and ability to execute boating rescue in a quick and effective manner in an emergency, he will be ineffective.

The skill sets required to supervise and execute rescue in a boating emergency are *very* different than those required to execute rescue of an individual in a swimming pool. Most lifeguard training focuses on rescue skills specific *only* to swimming activities, typically in the enclosed controlled environment of a swimming pool, and does not include any instruction on how to paddle, or how to execute any type of boating rescue. (Do you really want to have a person who can't paddle his own boat responsible for the speedy rescue of participants?)

Lifeguards who are not trained *specifically* in boat rescue skills can actually become an additional hazard in an emergency situation, and can endanger the lives of the participants, as well as their own. Lifeguards without competent paddling skills may not arrive to the victim in a timely manner, may hit victims in the water, or may capsize their own craft in the rescue attempt. These hazards are magnified in whitewater settings, as pool-trained lifeguards have little understanding of the risks of in-water hazards or the effects of current.

In order to use someone certified as a lifeguard in the supervision of boating activities, he should be additionally trained in paddling and rescue skills, and this should be specific to the type(s) of craft and bodies of water to be used.

Prior to Playing: Participant Safety

Participant Swimming Ability

All participants should have a level of comfort and swimming skills appropriate for the activities *in* the water before paddling *on* the water. It is highly recommended that a swimming skills evaluation be conducted prior to paddling activities taking place, including swimming while wearing a lifejacket. Each paddler (and any non-paddling passengers) should be able to demonstrate swimming ability that is sufficient to safely rescue themselves in the body of water they are paddling on, including the ability to swim underwater, in current, through rapids, or in surf as applicable.

Self-Rescue Skills

Participants should know how to execute self-rescue, be able to re-enter their canoe or kayak from in the water, and be able to assist others back into their boats. Self-rescue skills are some of the first on-water skills participants should learn, practice, and have mastered before they actually *need* use of these skills in a real event.

Safety Orientation

Prior to any on-water game play, supervisors should review safety requirements with participants, including, but not limited to:
- Emergency procedures to be followed, including what to do in the event of someone capsizing, and expectations for self-rescue and assisting others
- Activity-area boundaries, and any areas that are off-limits
- Expectations regarding the group staying together, distance between boats, and such
- Types of signals to be used for communication, such as whistles, hand signals, or flags. Be sure this signal includes a system for quickly recalling craft, audible and/or visual
- Identify any hazards in the area, along with instructions on avoidance
- What to do if they need assistance
- Rules for gear/equipment use (such as wearing lifejackets at all times, helmet use, etc.)
- "Rules of the road" for waterway traffic if applicable
- Game play conduct

Participant Health History

Boating activities can be very physically demanding. Some medical conditions pose additional risk—and can be life-threatening—in an aquatics environment, such as seizure disorders, heart conditions, respiratory problems, or conditions that may result in becoming unconscious underwater. Supervisors should be aware of all participant medical conditions, including any physical limitations which may impact full participation. It is recommended that each participant complete a health history prior to paddling. (Note that some organizations, such as camps and youth agencies, have specific standards for when health histories or physical health exams are required.)

Participants With Disabilities

Paddling is a sport that is adaptable for individuals with many types of physical abilities, usually without any (or very few) modifications to standard equipment. Under the Americans With Disabilities Act of 1990, a person may not be excluded from a program just because they have a disability. Program operators need to be prepared to integrate persons with disabilities into existing programs, and should provide training for instructors and supervisors to help ensure they are able to meet the needs of paddlers with disabilities, and do so safely. For more information on working with participants with disabilities, contact the American Canoe Association (www.americancanoe.org).

A Note About Setting Minimum Age Limits for Youth

Chronological age *alone* does not determine if a paddling activity is safe or appropriate for *any* individual—kids or adults. Factors *other than age*, such as comfort in and around the water, swimming skills, and physical ability to paddle, and so forth, must be taken into consideration when deciding if paddling activities are appropriate for *any* participant. After all, differences in attention spans, physical ability, coordination, swimming ability, physical development, and maturity can be found within any group. A teenager with a strong fear of the water or an adult with poor coordination are not going to be better—or safer—candidates for participation just because they have reached a particular age.

However, too often kids are arbitrarily left out of paddling activities simply based on a set minimum age requirement, rather than their actual ability to learn the material and paddle. Decisions to set minimum age limits for youth participants need to be made carefully. Ideally, the capacities of each individual child should be considered when determining if that child allowed to paddle, rather than this decision being based on age alone. With the right instruction, supervision, environment, and gear, even *very* young children can lean to paddle, and do so safely. Some factors to consider include:
- The child's emotional readiness and desire to participate
- The child's physical abilities and limitations
- The size of available equipment and gear

As required for any participant, each youth paddler should be able to demonstrate swimming ability that is sufficient to safely rescue themselves in the body of water they are paddling on, be physically able to execute self-rescue, and re-enter their canoe or kayak from in the water.

Prior to Playing: Gear

Lifejackets

Everyone paddling—including the people supervising the activities—must wear a properly fitting U.S. Coast Guard–approved lifejacket (PFD: personal flotation device) at all times when on the water.

Lifejackets provide additional flotation in case of an unexpected swim or capsize, as well as a layer of warmth in cold water. Certain life jackets are designed to keep paddlers' heads above water and help them remain in a position that permits proper breathing. Even strong swimmers should wear a lifejacket. To work correctly, a life jacket must be worn, fit snugly, and not allow the wearer's chin or ears to slip through. Youth swimmers should wear an appropriately fitting youth-sized lifejacket. State laws regarding lifejacket use vary by location. All states have regulations regarding lifejacket wear by children. Check with your local boating agency regarding requirements, or refer to the U.S. Coast Guard's Boating Safety Division (www.uscgboating.org) for additional information.

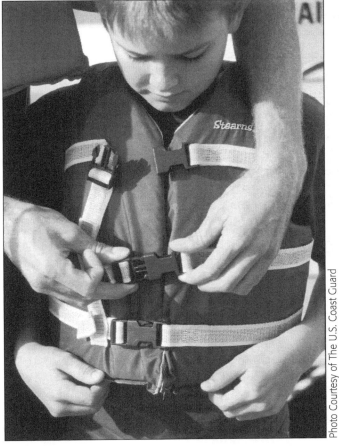

Photo Courtesy of The U.S. Coast Guard

Helmets

Boating helmets are designed to protect the paddler from head injuries. It is recommended that protective helmets be required to be worn:

- At all times when participants are paddling a decked boat, such as a whitewater kayak, or other type of decked boat or with an enclosed cockpit
- Whenever any type of restraint system is being utilized, such as thigh straps
- Any time a participant may have a chance of hitting his head on something hard, either above or below the surface, such as when paddling in areas with rocks, or on surf launchings and landings (Remember that hard objects are often found under water that you can't see from the surface.)
- Whenever practicing wet exits or rolls
- Paddlers in all types of craft whenever paddling in Class III or higher whitewater

Dress for Water Temperatures

Participants should be dressed for the water temperature. Exposure to cold water can cause hypothermia, which develops when the body cannot produce enough heat to maintain normal temperature. A layering system of clothing—comprised of wool or synthetic layers that are insulating even when wet, along with a windproof outer layer—is suggested, so participants can add or remove layers for comfort. A hat and gloves should be added in colder conditions. When the water temperature is 55 degrees Fahrenheit or below, or when the water temperature combined with the air temperature is less than 100 degrees Fahrenheit, a wet suit or dry suit should be required.

Safety Check for Boats

Do not use boats that are unsafe. Before going out on the water, make sure that all canoes and kayaks are in good repair, are outfitted properly for water conditions, and are in compliance with any local, state, or federal regulations if required. Canoes should have end lines (painters). Be sure to consider weather and water conditions, and the weight of the passengers and equipment, and do not exceed the craft's maximum weight and capacity.

To help prevent entrapment emergencies, check any boats with an enclosed cockpit to ensure that the cockpit size is appropriate to the size of the user, and that the paddler can exit the craft easily in the event of capsize. Additionally, kayaks should have reinforced decks—back and front (check for foam panels or flotation).

Check for sharp edges, cracks, points, breaks, protruding rivets, or anything else that could cause the paddler to get caught, or cut, on either the inside or outside of the boat. This precaution is especially important with aluminum canoes, and aluminum parts on any boat, as cracked or broken metal can be *very* sharp and result in serious injuries.

A Note About Safe Equipment

Many older model aluminum canoes—specifically those made in the period between the 1940s and the 1960s, which are still in use in many youth programs and summer camps—were made with foam blocks encased under the bow and stern deck plates. The manufacturer's design of many of these older canoes is such that they were not built to float when capsized *unless* the foam is fully intact. However, as the foam disintegrates with age (and often becomes home to insects), it is common to discover little, if any, of the original foam left. It can be a sudden, unexpected, and disturbing surprise when one of these canoes flips over, and promptly sinks—often quickly going straight to the bottom of the lake. People working with older canoes should check the foam flotation as part of the boat safety check. Replace the missing foam with new foam block, or use polyurethane spray foam insulation, which will expand to fill the cavity with a semi-rigid closed cell foam mass, which does not degrade or shrink.

What Else to Take Along?

In addition to the boat, lifejacket, and paddle, the other items participants need to have with them will vary depending on the location, length of activity, as well as weather and water conditions. A group of kids paddling for a few hours on a flatwater pond on a sunny day while at summer camp are going to have different gear needs than those paddling on a three-day river trip after a spring dam release. Have the following items available, or advise individual paddlers to bring the following, as applicable:

- Drinking water, snacks
- Sunscreen, sunglasses, or other sun protection, as well as insect repellent
- Appropriate clothing, including footwear, and change(s) of clothing (stored in a waterproof bag)
- Clothing for changes in weather, including raingear that is safe when worn with a lifejacket
- Any other personal gear needed for paddling (e.g., spray skirt, helmet, kneepads, whistle)

The people supervising activities should have the following:
- Supplies for the games and activities to be played
- Emergency action plan(s)
- Health history for each participant (Be aware of any participant medical conditions.)
- First aid supplies, including personal protective equipment, that are appropriate to the location, length of activity, and number of participants
- Rescue equipment as applicable to the craft/water (throw bags, river knife, rope, etc.)

- Knowledge of the waterway(s) where you plan to play, including any issues with access, emergency response, hazards, or any other factors that might affect safe boating
- Weather information
- Access to safe drinking water (as well as meals/snacks, if these are to be provided)
- Access to restroom facilities, or alternatives that are environmentally responsible and follow a "leave no trace" philosophy

Be Prepared for Emergencies

Depending on the activities conducted, participants served, and paddling location, supervisors should have emergency action plans, first aid supplies, and emergency supplies for the following situations:
- Medical emergencies (minor and major)
- Getting caught out on the water at dusk/dark, or a sudden change in visibility, such as fog
- Sudden weather changes or severe weather
- Being unable to call for help, or if emergency medical services cannot get to you

Prior to Playing: Selecting an Appropriate Body of Water

To help ensure safe and appropriate places to paddle and play, on-water activity areas should be selected by considering the skill level of participants, degree of risk, and environmental conditions.

Select Locations That Are Suitable to the Skill Level of the Participants

Only paddle where water conditions are suitable to the skill level of the participants. When working with beginners, the ideal location for instruction and game play will be on calm, flat water, in an area protected from wind, waves, and wakes, such as a pond or a protected cove on a lake. Remember that novice paddlers will have both limited ability to control their boat, and are most at risk of accidental capsizing, so try to select a location with plenty of room to maneuver, and as few underwater hazards as possible to reduce the risk of injury if they capsize. As participants progress in their paddling skills and gain better boat control, they will be able to better react and respond to the effects of wind and variations in water conditions, such as currents, and may progress to paddling on waterways which offer more challenge.

When paddling on moving water, supervisors must select locations where participants' paddle within their limits, as well as those of the group's. Only paddle where participants are able to "read" the water and effectively steer and propel their boat. Again, it is critical to *only* paddle where water conditions are suitable to the skill level of the participants, and to select areas where participants can easily keep their boats under control.

As an additional safety practice, it is recommended that participants paddle at *least* one class level of difficulty *below* the paddling and rescue ability of the people supervising the activities. For example, if the people supervising activities are competent paddlers and instructors in Class II whitewater, participants should paddle nothing higher than Class I.

Be Aware of Hazards

For all types of water, pay attention to features and hazards that can be seen both above and below the water. These features include natural hazards, such as submerged rocks and downed trees, as well as man-made hazards, such as water-leveling drains on ponds, underwater pipes, dams, and such. Be sure to consider water conditions, including water clarity, as well as any currents, tides, wave height, wind speed, surf zones, or other features. Also, know if the level and class of water is controlled or impacted by dam release. Water temperature and weather conditions may also be hazard factors. For safety, try to select locations that are free from as many hazards as possible.

When possible, try to avoid areas with other boat traffic. If motorized watercraft is operating nearby, be sure participants know when to stop playing, and to turn their bow into the wave to help prevent capsize, rather than taking the wake motions broadside.

In moving water, set up your playing areas well away from any hazards, such as strainers, undercut rocks, bridge pilings, low-head dams, hydraulics, and such. Look downstream for anything that may become a hazard if a participant were to capsize or otherwise wind up downstream. When playing in rapids, always "scout" the section before running it, and have appropriate safety set up and ready before play as applicable. Participants should never enter a rapid that they are unable to swim (the entire rapid) in the event of capsize.

Access to the Waterway

Before selecting a location, be aware of any issues regarding access to the waterway and use. Know if access points are open to the public, or if you have to cross private property, and if so, the permission required from landowners (never trespass to gain access). Consider any challenges in getting to the waterway, such as difficult terrain or hazards such as having to cross railroad tracks or walk through poison ivy, parking problems, and the like. Some waterways require a permit, license, or use sticker on the boat. Be sure to check required compliance with any local, state, or federal regulations.

Access to, and by, Emergency Medical Services

It is not unusual in outdoor recreational settings to not have the option to call 911 for emergency assistance, especially in remote locations. When selecting a location, know if you can contact help in an emergency, and be sure to take into consideration the time it takes for either emergency medical services to get to you, or for you to get the victim to EMS. Also, be aware that in some locations, it may not be possible for EMS to get to you. Decisions to paddle and play in locations where EMS access is slow, limited, or not possible must be made carefully, with considerations given to the type of clientele served, as well as the qualifications and abilities of the people supervising the activities to handle emergency medical situations without additional professional assistance.

Ease of Rescue

When selecting a location, it is important to assess how easy it will be to execute rescue in a quick and effective manner in the event of capsize, medical emergency, or other situation when fast access to a participant is critical. For example, water conditions, such as currents, tides, and waves, as well as wind speed, may impact the ease and speed it takes for the rescue craft to arrive and assist the victim. Water temperature, water clarity, as well as natural and man-made hazards should also be considered.

Also, consider how you will organize the activities and keep the group together while playing. For safety, consider keeping the playing area small enough so that rescue can be executed quickly in the event of an emergency.

On some bodies of water, or for some activities, it may be important to have access to features where supervisors can be stationed in order to set up and be prepared for rescue, such as standing on a large stable rock or sandbar at the ready with a throw-bag at a rapid. Again, when on moving water or whitewater, to help ensure effective rescue, it is highly recommended that participants paddle at *least* one class level of difficulty *below* the rescue skills ability of those supervising the activities.

Know the Rules of the Road

Know the laws, restrictions, and "rules of the road" applicable for the waterway(s) utilized. This factor is specifically important when paddling in areas with commercial boating traffic, military vessels, motorized watercraft, and when around some shore-based facilities, such as power plants. Respect Homeland Security protection zones, and stay at least 100 yards away from all naval vessels, military installations, piers, and other security zones. For additional information, consult the U.S. Coast Guard regulations, or contact local law enforcement.

Creature Comforts

When selecting a location, consider the "creature comforts" for participants, such as access to restrooms, drinking water, places to change clothing, and shelter in the event of inclement weather.

When restroom facilities are not available, you will need an alternative which is environmentally responsible. Follow "leave no trace" ethics, and use an approved method to pack out solid human waste and paper products. Many waterways require the use of a portable toilet, which must be transported with the group. Dispose of liquid waste at least 200 feet away from the water, or follow the disposal requirements for the waterway. Consult with the appropriate local, state, or federal waterway or resource management enforcement office for additional information.

Use of Swimming Pools for Boating Activities

Swimming pools can be very appealing for conducting boating activities, as they provide an easily controlled location and good water clarity, and they are free from various hazards found in natural environments. The use of an indoor pool further offers opportunities for paddling on rainy days or during winter months in colder climates.

Note the potential for increased risk of head injury when boating in a swimming pool, and the use of helmets for protection is recommended. The close proximity of boats to other boats as well the hard surface edge of the pool can result in paddlers hitting their head when capsizing. Without a lot of space to maneuver, those participants who fall in the water may also be struck in the head by a boat trying to paddle out of the way. As a matter of preventing head injuries from occurring, swimmers and boaters should not be in the water at the same time.

Steps should also be taken to protect the swimming pool as well, as canoes and kayaks running in to the sides, steps, and railings can cause damage. Plastic or inflatable boats should be used when possible. Soft padding, such as foam, towels, or a discarded lifejacket, can be attached to the bow and stern ends with duct tape to help protect the pool from impact.

iStockphoto/Thinkstock

2

Using Games and Activities in Instruction

Photo Courtesy of The U.S. Coast Guard

Playing helps facilitate a dynamic learning process. Participants are more likely to enjoy and return to an activity they had fun doing—and they are probably going to learn more in a fun and playful setting as well.

Games aren't boring; they get to the point of learning by participating and doing. A key point to mastering and retaining a new motor skill is practice. By including games and activities in your curriculum, you provide opportunities for participants to put new skills into practice, and to do so in a fun way. Playing is a more relaxed way of practicing skills, where participants are not "overthinking" but rather are engaged "in the doing." While playing, participants are often thinking less about the individual strokes, and actually feeling the effect they have on the boat more.

Adding games is a good way to add variety to the curriculum in order to keep your participants interested and help prevent boredom. Playing games helps to keep participants engaged in learning, which increases the opportunity for participants to progress in their skills. (Being ready with some extra games in your "bag of tricks" will also be helpful incase the participants get through the planned activity quicker than anticipated, or the other activities planned that day bombed.)

Selecting Games and Activities to Use

When used in an instructional setting, the game or activity selected should be connected to the specific learning to be accomplished. Think of the games and activities as skill builders that will be used to reinforce the strokes and maneuvers you are teaching. In some cases, the games can be the instructional delivery method, targeting a specific skill. In other cases, the activities equate to a fun alternative to traditional skills drills.

Be sure participants are ready for the game or activity. Select games that are appropriate to the skills and abilities of participants. Look at what they can and cannot do. For success, make sure participants are able to at least fundamentally execute all of the skills, strokes, or maneuvers required to meet the game objectives. They don't all have to be able to paddle at the same *level* of skill, but do need to have the *ability to perform* the skills. Activities that are too challenging will only serve to frustrate paddlers.

Remember that the paddlers who will benefit the most from skills practice will be the lesser-skilled paddlers, so it's important to keep them participating and playing games where they have success. (Note that the tag games in this book are intentionally designed so that those players who are tagged are not "out" of the game, but rather they continue to participate, often in a changed role as a player, in order to help ensure adequate paddling time.)

The level of play should be appropriate to both the paddling abilities and physical condition of the participants. Be prepared to vary the length and intensity of activities, and don't expect the same level of playing capacity from everyone.

In addition to paddling skills, supervisors must consider the differences between participants—such as attention spans, coordination, emotional intelligence, physical development, and emotional maturity—when deciding which games and activities to play. When working with kids, remember that the level of concentration required to participate should be appropriate for the ages of the paddlers.

While physical safety should be the number one priority during paddlesports activities, supervisors must also take emotional safety into consideration, especially around game play that includes competition. Always be aware of the emotional and physical limits—and limitations—of participants. Be aware of the energy level of the group as well.

Pacing

People supervising boating activities should always be prepared to vary the intensity of the activity or game, and be ready to make changes. The pace of the game should change with the needs of the participants. If paddlers are starting to tire, take a break, change to a new activity, or modify the current activity by changing things like the boundaries, rules, equipment, number of players, teams, etc. If it's a game they really like and want to play again, try to mix it up and come back to that game later, so no one "burns out" from playing the same thing too many times. Always try to end the game before it ends itself; end while the energy level, and interest, is still high.

Considering Competition

Competition in game play is a double-edged sword. On one side will be participants for whom competition creates fear, anxiety, and stress, which can cripple their ability to learn and perform, thus defeating the whole instructional purpose. On the other side will be participants who thrive on performing in a competitive environment, and some participants may even become bored and disengage from learning without it.

When the game or activity is for the purpose of facilitating effective learning, using competitive game play can be a real instructional challenge, as it is easy to *totally* miss the learning objective when paddlers are participating in a competitive game. Participants may become so focused on winning or keeping up with the boat in front of them that practicing or improving any specific paddling skill is lost.

For those participants who don't learn well, or "shut down" in a competitive setting, emotions such as tension, timidity, and anxiety are realities that those supervising must consider when deciding which games to play, and if they are going to be conducted in a competitive manner. Be aware that competition may discourage and frustrate lesser-skilled paddlers. (Note that this reaction is often an indicator that more paddling instruction and practice time is needed to build skills and confidence *before* playing.)

To help ensure that game play is both fun and fair—and that you don't discourage anyone—consider pairing participants who have higher level paddling skills with those with lesser level skills. It's also good to mix the teams up and change them often. This approach will help level the playing field and prevent domination by a few paddlers.

It may be appropriate to couch competition in a way that encourages paddlers to "compete" with themselves; to improve their paddling skills and judge their performance on their own progress, rather than judging their performance by comparing their skills to others. Trying to beat their own time or to reduce the number of strokes it takes to complete a maneuver are good ways for paddlers to compete with themselves.

Instructors must also recognize that competition may push some participants to try to paddle beyond their paddling ability or their level of emotional comfort, creating both physical and emotional safety issues. For safety, it may be appropriate at times for a game or activity to be conducted at the level of the *least-skilled* paddler in the group, such as when participants might feel "pushed" to paddle, or to take risks in attempting skills, beyond their ability.

Get Them Out on the Water

Don't kill your program by talking the participants to death. They don't want to stand around, listening to you talk about what they *might* be doing; they want to get out there and *do* it. A common mistake of rookie instructors is to get so bogged down in giving out information that the majority of the activity time is taken up by the instructor, with very little time on the water for the participants. They came to paddle, so let them do it.

Length of Activity Time

In order to have success, it's important to have enough time to conduct activities. Participants in boating programs typically have to do a variety of tasks before and after they paddle, such as putting on lifejackets, changing clothes, moving equipment, moving boats, and such. The time the participants have to *actually* paddle should be carefully balanced with the time required to arrive, get ready, have instruction, move boats, and clean up at the end.

Okay, So That Game Bombed

It is impossible to predict what will happen with every group you work with. Every group is different, so the same lesson plan is not going to work all the time, and not every game is going to work for all paddlers. Try to remember that the activities are important *only* if they help in meeting the learning objectives. If you overhear one of the participants say something like, "This game sucks," take it as an indicator that a change is needed. If one game doesn't work, don't take it personally. It happens; simply change what you are doing.

Also, remember that the *whole* lesson plan should facilitate a dynamic learning process! If you don't get a sense that participants think this was the coolest thing ever, go back and look at what instruction is being provided and how. Assuming that the problem is not caused by staff (poor attitude, not paying enough attention to the participants, being a "fun killer"), and look at the elements that are "fun" in your lesson plans. Remove or alter the delivery of anything that is a "wet blanket" to your program. Be creative (while keeping the activities safe), and find ways to keep the participants engaged and happy.

Photo Courtesy of The U.S. Coast Guard

But That's Not How I Learned It

Each paddlesports instructional organization and instructor certification program retains and teaches its own unique curriculum. Thus, the content, terminology, and manner in which some of the strokes and maneuvers are instructed will vary. Additionally, a lot of diversity is found in how instructors, trainers, and educators teach the various paddlesports curriculums. The people instructing material in this book may find differences in the content, which is not the same as how it may have been presented in a prior course. When this discrepancy occurs, instructors should teach the material they are familiar with, and/or in the manner outlined by their specific certifying body as applicable. Additionally, as a matter of respecting the variations between curriculums, some of the activities found in this book will not define the specific strokes to be taught and/or sequencing to be practiced in order to execute a maneuver. Rather, this aspect is left to the discretion of the instructor.

3

Set-Up and Supplies

Prior to Playing: Boundaries and Safe Play

Setting Up the Playing Area

For safety, it is important to establish a playing area that is easily supervised, and where rescue can be executed quickly in the event of an emergency.

Some of the games and activities require boundaries for the playing area, in order to keep the group together and organized. The size of the playing area will vary based on the specific activity, the number of boats, types of boats, skill level of the paddlers, body of water, and how challenging you want to make the activity. Establishing the area can be as simple as drawing imaginary lines between fixed objects, such as from the end of a dock to a tree on the shoreline, or with physical markers such as paddling between rocks, or with the use of buoys.

Many of the games require a large open area, so paddlers can maneuver past each other easily, without colliding into each other or into other objects such as bridges or docks. Be sure to have a clear zone around the outside of the playing area as well, in case a boat is unable to stop inside the boundary. This aspect is especially important around end zones or goal lines.

Contact, Collisions, and Capsizing

While boating is not typically a contact sport, it is not uncommon for some contact to occur between boats, paddles, and people during game play (and it's not unusual for this type of contact to increase during competitive play).

Paddle Contact: Paddle-to-paddle, paddle-to-boat, or paddle-to-person contact is most likely to occur during activities where boats are in close proximity, during highly competitive play, or when objects, such as balls, are being thrown from boat to boat.

Be aware of the potential for participants to use paddles to deflect objects, boats, and other paddlers:

- Discourage the use of paddles as "bats."
- Set limits for how high a paddle may be lifted and used out of the water, similar to hockey where "high sticking" is called as a penalty.
- Enforce rules that paddles may not be used as a tool (or weapon) to deflect other people or other boats.

You may have times when it is a wise idea for participants to wear helmets, such as when experienced paddlers are playing team sports like #30: Dead Fish Polo—especially if you are dealing with highly competitive personalities. Another option if you only have kayaks in a group is to take away the paddles and have everyone hand-paddle, thus reducing both the speed of play, as well as the opportunity for paddle-to-noggin contact.

Collisions: Collisions are most common with novice paddlers, who typically have less boat control, and so may be unable to stop or maneuver to avoid hitting another boat. A larger playing area may help prevent collisions, as it gives lesser-skilled paddlers more time to react and room to maneuver. Be aware that collisions by and between experienced boaters can sometimes be intentional, as one paddler tries to "take out" a competitor by pushing the other out of the way or by capsizing the other boat (or they may collide with the intention of a pirate-style boarding and capture, often followed by an intentional capsizing). For safety, clear rules of play should be established and boat-to-boat contact discouraged.

Capsizing: Capsizing during play is also not uncommon, *and its inevitability should be planned for*. In a safe setting, a capsize may provide a teachable moment and a good opportunity for participants to practice their rescue skills. Participants should know what to do not only if their own boat capsizes, but also what the expectations are when it's another boat. Questions to be considered and planned for include:
- Does game play stop when a boat capsizes?
- How will this stopping of game play be communicated to everyone?
- Who is responsible to assist and rescue? How is this responsibility determined?
- Do the other paddlers stop in place, or should they go somewhere to wait?

When Canoes and Kayaks Are Mixed Together in Play

Special consideration needs to be taken when both kayaks and canoes are paddling and playing in the same location, especially when boats are in close proximity. Kayakers who are hit directly by a canoe can suffer serious injuries. Because of their size, canoes can easily slide over the top (deck) of many kayaks. This possibility may be a critical safety concern if the kayak has capsized and the paddler is unable to roll back to the surface because a canoe is sitting on top of the boat. While inexperienced paddlers with limited boat control are most at risk of accidentally running over a fellow boater, aggressive play by experienced boaters can also have the same result. To help prevent injury:
- Make paddlers aware, and discuss the need to paddle "in control."
- Enforce "no boat ramming" rules in game play.
- Enlarge the playing area so boats have more space to maneuver, or reduce the number of boats.
- Consider separating canoes from kayaks, specifically for those activities where boats may come in contact, or when competitive paddlers are playing a little aggressively.

Supplies

Some of the games and activities require basic supplies. The specific items needed are listed with each game and activity. All of the items listed for game play in this book are easily found in places like toy stores, dollar stores, hardware stores, or discount marts. Physical education or recreation supply catalogs are also good sources for supplies.

Remember that whatever goes out on the water should float. When in doubt, test your toys in the bathtub first. Ideally, try to purchase items that are waterproof, and remember that some items, such as blindfolds, will need to be washable. Plan your supplies with the idea that everything *will* get wet, and think about how to protect and preserve items at the front end. Doing so will help save both time and money in having to purchase the same supplies twice or from having to go back and make the boat parts flashcards over again because they got ruined. Plastic zipper-lock baggies are great for storing items which need to be kept dry. Mesh net bags are good for keeping toys organized and for storage of wet toys, as the netting allows for air to circulate around the items.

Consider Unpredictable Equipment

The use of traditional familiar sports equipment, such as a football, tends to bring out a predictable mindset in participants. Those participants who are adept at sports will embrace the activity, while those who are not will feel an additional level of stress and performance anxiety. Objects other than traditional sports equipment, such as rubber ducks, balloons, and fish-shaped sponges, are handy because they don't automatically imply a need to "be good at sports" in order to participate.

Throwables

Many of the games require throwables, objects that can be thrown from boat to boat during the course of play. All throwables should be small enough, and light enough, that they don't hurt anyone if they happen to hit a participant when thrown. Some suggested items include:
- Rubber ducks
- Sponge balls (in various sizes and shapes)
- Plastic hollow street hockey balls (*not* the solid heavy plastic ones)
- Sponges (the larger car cleaning size, as well as the smaller household size)
- Plastic perforated baseballs or golf balls
- Beach balls
- Rubber deck tennis rings
- Hollow plastic fruit

Because of the risk of injury with contact, try to avoid the use hard balls, such as baseballs and softballs, or larger items, such as soccer balls and volleyballs.

Other Items

The specific supplies required are listed with each game and activity. Additionally, it is a good idea for the instructor(s) to have a whistle.

Buoys

It is recommended that you have at least four to six floating buoys. They can be set out to mark the corners of the playing area, and be used as goalposts, objects to turn around, and such.

Many sources are available for either purchasing or making buoys. An empty plastic gallon jug with a lid and handle, such as a milk jug, works great. Simply attach one end of the line through the handle, and the other to the weight, which can be a large rock, brick, or cinder block. (Refrain from recycling bleach bottles, detergent bottles, or other chemical product bottles as buoys, as any remaining cleaning product or chemicals could pose a hazard to the aquatic habitat.)

Inflatable vinyl buoys are available from marine supply or boating pro shops. Swimming pool rope floats will also work as markers, and can be found in a pool supply store or catalog. Many toy stores sell a large inflatable ball with a handle, the kind used by kids to hop around on, which also works great as a buoy. For people looking for a more whimsical option, floating alligator decoys, hippo heads, and the like are available from garden supply and pond supply stores. Designed to be placed in koi ponds to protect the fish from being eaten, or to keep geese out of lakes and ponds, these fun floats make for great buoys in paddling activities.

PART 2

THE GAMES AND ACTIVITIES

4

Games and Activities for Building On-Water Confidence

Please note that many of the activities in this chapter are also suitable to be used in conjunction with self-rescue instruction and activities found in Chapter 5.

Let Them Get Wet

Provided that the waterway is not infested with piranha, swimming is permitted, the lake is not frozen over, and participants can be monitored in a safe manner, let your paddlers get wet. While activities that include swimming may *seem* counterintuitive to paddling instruction, many benefits can result from participants playing around *in* the water as part of a boating instructional program.

Activities that include tipping over, hopping out, and climbing back in can help participants build a better sense of balance, increase confidence in the craft, and improve their physical relationship in the boat as they test the craft's stability. Spending time playing with the boats in the water helps to prepare participants for learning in-water self-rescue skills. These types of activities also help participants gain a better understanding of how the design of the boat impacts the performance capacity of the craft.

Additionally, depending on the clientele served, in-water play may be an important first step in helping participants become comfortable around, on, and in the body of water. Those participants new to paddlesports often have fears and misconceptions about the stability of boats. Some individuals simply don't like being on water where they can't see the bottom, or have a fear of the mysterious unknown critters they imagine lurking in the water, just wondering what freshly-capsized paddler tastes like. For these participants, this in-water time can be critically important, in the very least, in helping prevent fear and panic in the event of accidental capsize.

Safety Reminders

- Everyone participating in in-water games and activities should be wearing a properly fitting U.S. Coast Guard–approved lifejacket at all times.
- Supervisors should know the swimming ability and in-water comfort level for all participants. It is highly recommended that a swimming skills evaluation be conducted prior to in-water activities taking place, including swimming while wearing a lifejacket.
- Pay attention to the water temperature, as well as the air temperature, and be sure participants are dressed appropriately.
- Kayakers (and any other paddlers with decked boats or enclosed cockpits) must have the ability to, minimally, execute a wet-exit prior to participating.

#1: Slow-Motion

Craft: Tandem or solo canoes

Skill Level: Any

Water: Calm flatwater, ideally without wind or waves

Playing Area: Clear open area, large enough so boats can be spaced apart and do not come in contact

Supplies: Boats

Skills: Balance, confidence in the canoe, understanding of craft's stability. If tandem, also builds communication and trust.

The goal of this activity is to capsize the canoe as *slowly*, and with as little motion, as possible. Typically, when paddlers are trying to flip a canoe over for an intentional capsize, they will rapidly rock the canoe with lots of gusto, using a lot of force and energy to get it to tip over. In this activity, paddlers should try to use as little force as possible as they try to accomplish a controlled capsize in slow-motion.

An outcome of this activity is that paddlers gain a better understanding of the initial and secondary stability of the canoe they are paddling. The slowing down allows for the participants to really feel how the boat is responding to their motions and actions. Many will discover that it is a lot harder to tip a canoe than they may have imagined. For some new to canoeing, this is a confidence-building, "a-ha" moment, as they realize the canoe isn't just going to tip over and feed them to the fishes for no reason.

Photo Courtesy of The U.S. Coast Guard

#2: Seal Races

Craft: Solo kayaks
Skill Level: Any
Water: Flatwater
Playing Area: Clear open area
Supplies: Kayaks (No paddles required, as participants are hand-paddling.)
Skills: Balance, in-water confidence, fundamentals in boat control, understanding of craft's stability
Note: Kayaks should have smooth hulls.

For this game, you will need to establish start and finish lines. Kayaks start in upright position, with participants in the water at the stern end. Have participants arrange boats so that bows are on the start line, facing the direction of the finish line, with four to six feet between boats.

At the start signal, participants climb on top of the hull and lie face down, with their arms and legs extending into the water (like they would when paddling a surfboard), and swim-paddle the boat to the finish line as fast as possible. If they fall off, they should reboard and continue. The first seal to cross the line wins.

#3: Flippers Up

Craft: Solo kayaks
Skill Level: Any
Water: Flatwater
Playing Area: Clear open area
Supplies: Kayaks (No paddles required as participants are hand-paddling.)
Skills: Balance, in-water confidence, fundamentals in boat control, understanding of craft's stability
Note: Kayaks should have smooth hulls.

The set-up is a modified version of #2: Seal Races. Before playing, establish a visual or auditory signal, which will tell the participants to swim-paddle ("flippers in") and stop ("flippers up"). Start the race, allowing the seals to swim forward, then show the stop ("flippers up") signal, at which time they must pull their flippers (arms and legs) out of the water and drift. Of course, doing so will result in boats turning and spinning as they drift along. After allowing for whatever drifting you want, call the "flippers in" signal, allowing them to resume their swim-paddling. Continue alternating the "flippers in" and "flippers up" signals as often as you want. If they fall off, they should reboard and continue. The first seal to cross the line wins.

#4: Trust Lean

Craft: Tandem canoes

Skill Level: Any

Water: Calm flatwater, ideally without wind or waves

Playing Area: Clear open area, large enough so boats can be spaced apart and do not come in contact

Supplies: Canoes

Skills: Partner communication, trust, balance, confidence, understanding of craft's stability

Note: Capsizing during this activity is common, and should be planned for.

Canoes start at a standstill in open area, spaced apart from each other so they do not come in contact. Paddles are stowed, hands are free, and the paddlers are in a seated position on bow and stern seats (rather than kneeling). One paddler moves at a time (it does not matter if the bow or stern paddler moves first). While staying seated, one paddler rotates on the seat from facing forward to facing sideways, placing feet and legs over the gunwale so they are outside of the boat. Once finished moving, the other paddler does the same, however, they rotate the opposite direction so that their feet and legs are over the opposite gunwale. At this point, paddlers should be facing sideways in the opposite direction; one paddler's legs will be over the port side, the other's will be over the starboard side.

Next, they each need to slowly lie back, so that their bodies are parallel with the surface of the water and their heads are now outside of the canoe as well. Once situated, they, together, begin rocking the boat from side to side (gunwale to gunwale)—one will be going feet-to-head, while the other is going head-to-feet. This motion will require communication between the paddlers. The goal is to get the canoe rocking from gunwale to gunwale where paddlers get both their feet wet and the top of their heads wet with each rocking motion, and doing so without flipping the canoe over. (For canoes without seats, paddlers can position themselves between thwarts. Some paddlers may find success by moving closer to the center of the canoe.)

One "full rock" is from starboard, where one paddler gets his feet wet and the other one gets the top of his head wet, to port, where one paddler gets his feet wet and the other one gets the top of his head wet. Give participants a goal for the number of full rocks to do in a row, or increase the challenge by setting a minimum number of full rocks to be completed in a set time. A modified version is to have paddlers rotate in the same manner, but instead keep their feet and legs inside of the canoe. This option requires paddlers to rest more of their weight on the gunwale and to commit more of their upper body to the outside of the boat.

#5: Leapfrog

Craft: Tandem canoes

Skill Level: Any

Water: Calm flatwater, ideally without wind or waves

Playing Area: Clear open area, large enough so boats can be spaced apart and do not come in contact

Supplies: Canoes

Skills: Partner communication, trust, balance, confidence, understanding of craft's stability

Note: Capsize during this activity is common, and should be planned for.

The game is called Leapfrog because of the position one paddler takes "hopping" over the other as they switch places in the canoe. Prior to playing, participants should have instruction on changing positions in the canoe, and have had an opportunity to practice these skills.

For this game, you will need to establish start and finish lines. These lines need to be a good long distance apart. Have participants arrange boats so that bows are on the start line, facing the direction of the finish line, with about 10 feet between boats.

At the start signal, participants begin racing toward the end line. As desired, the instructor yells "Leapfrog," at which time the participants must pull their paddles out of the water, and change positions. Once they have completed the change, they may resume paddling. Again, the instructor yells "Leapfrog," and they have to repeat the switching process. Call "Leapfrog" as often as desired. The first canoe to cross the line wins.

If you don't have a lot of space or want to vary the play, modify the game by having partners switch positions at a set interval of strokes, such as after every six or every 10 strokes. This activity can also be played as an ongoing game throughout the day, where every time the instructor calls out "Leapfrog," participants have to change positions.

#6: Ants on a Log

Craft: Canoes ("logs"), with a minimum of four participants ("ants") per boat
Skill Level: Any
Water: Calm flatwater, ideally without wind or waves
Playing Area: Clear open area, large enough so boats can be spaced apart and do not come in contact
Supplies: Canoes
Skills: Partner communication, trust, balance, confidence, understanding of craft's stability
Note: Capsizing during this activity is common, and should be planned for.

Canoe starts at a standstill. The object of this activity is to switch positions so that all participants end up in the opposite position in the canoe from where they started, and do so without tipping the boat over. For example, the paddler in the stern seat will end up in the bow seat, and so forth. Allow paddlers to figure out their own solutions, as the objective can be met in multiple ways. As skills progress, try six people, three at each end, then eight, taking care not to overload the weight capacity of the canoe. This game can also be used as a teambuilding activity.

#7: People Paddle

Craft: None
Skill Level: Any
Water: Swimming pool or calm flatwater, ideally without wind or waves
Playing Area: Clear open area, large enough so swimming can be spaced apart
Supplies: Kayak paddles
Skills: Effect of paddle motion, flexibility, warm-up, in-water confidence

This activity is a swimming-while-paddling game. Have a start line and a finish line. Participants start standing holding a kayak paddle horizontally in front of them with both hands. At the signal to go, participants float on their backs with the paddle across their stomach, and paddle feet-first to the end line. For variation, try paddling forward while floating on stomach.

#8: Slip'n'Slide

Craft: Kayaks
Skill Level: Any
Water: Calm flatwater, ideally without wind or waves
Playing Area: Gentle gradual slope, which drops out in a clear open area of the water
Supplies: Kayaks
Skills: In-water confidence, getting a feel for the craft, improving balance
Note: Hillside should be smooth, free from rocks, stumps, or the like, which could damage the kayak.

In this activity, paddlers take a fun ride in their kayak down the hill. Load paddlers in their kayaks one at a time at the top of the slope and allow them to slide down the hill, ending up in the water. Participants can go without paddles and hand-paddle once they are in the water, or have them slide with paddles in hand. Running a water hose or throwing a couple of buckets of water down the slope will usually make it a little slicker and quicker. For safety, the hillside used should be a gradual slope, without any sudden drop-off where a kayak could become vertical before entering the water. Helmets and lifejackets should be worn by all participants in case the boat capsizes upon entry.

#9: Backwards Bugs

Craft: Solo kayaks
Skill Level: Any
Water: Flatwater
Playing Area: Clear open area
Supplies: Kayaks (No paddles required as participants are hand-paddling.)
Skills: Balance, in-water confidence, fundamentals in boat control, understanding of craft's stability

For this game, you will need to establish start and finish lines. Have participants arrange boats so that sterns are on the start line, facing the direction of the finish line, with four to six feet between boats. To get into the backwards bug position, participants climb on to the kayak and sit facing the bow, with their backside resting inside the cockpit, and legs on the outside. Then, they lay the rest of the body back, so that they are lying backwards on top of the boat, head down on the deck, looking up at the sky. (Participants can use their legs to help balance or as "rudders" to help in steering.)

At the start signal, participants backward hand-paddle the boat to the finish line as fast as possible. The first bug to cross the line wins. Vary the game by having participants try paddling the boat the other direction, heading feet first.

Upside-Down Canoe Games

In these activities, participants will discover that canoes can be fun not only right side up! These games help paddlers build a 360-degree relationship within the craft, prepare for self-rescue instruction, build in-water confidence, and also teach participants not to panic if they happen to surface inside of their upside down canoe after capsize.

Those supervising need to pay close attention to what is going on below the surface and under the boats. Limiting the number of boats that are upside down at any one time, as well as the number of participants, will help in keeping track of everyone.

When turned upside down, a canoe will have a large air pocket underneath. In these activities, participants go underneath the boat, using the air pocket to breath. The more buoyancy the canoe has, the "higher" it sits on the water, which typically increases the size of the air pocket. Canoes used for these activities must be in good condition, with adequate flotation and buoyancy. Consider adding additional flotation as needed.

Note: Depending on the specific type and design, some kayaks may be suitable to be used for these activities. Instructors should test the kayak upside down prior to playing to ensure it is appropriate to be used in this manner. Modify the activity so that there is only one participant per cockpit.

#10: Sing Down

Craft: Canoes (Games are suitable for two to four participants per boat, unless noted otherwise.)

Skill Level: Any

Water: Calm flatwater, deep enough for participants to stand at shoulder depth or deeper

Playing Area: Clear open area, but small enough to easily monitor

Supplies: Canoes

Skills: Build in-water confidence

Note: Be sure to instruct participants to keep their hands and fingers inside the upside-down boat, using the thwarts to push and "drive." This technique will help prevent finger injuries if boats collide.

A good introductory activity to being underneath the boat for the first time. Once everyone is underneath their boats, have them sing a song in unison. Those really obnoxious camp songs are good for this activity—the louder the better. Depending on the group you are working with, if you really want to throw out a challenge, have them try singing a round.

#11: Turtle Races

Craft: Canoes (Games are suitable for two to four participants per boat, unless noted otherwise.)

Skill Level: Any

Water: Calm flatwater, deep enough for participants to stand at shoulder depth or deeper

Playing Area: Clear open area, but small enough to easily monitor

Supplies: Canoes

Skills: In-water confidence

Note: Be sure to instruct participants to keep their hands and fingers inside the upside-down boat, using the thwarts to push and "drive." This technique will help prevent finger injuries if boats collide.

For this game, you will need to establish start and finish lines. Canoes start in upside-down position, and participants are in the water. Assign two to four participants per canoe. At the start line, have participants arrange canoes so that bows are on the start line, facing the direction of the finish line, with at least four to six feet between boats.

At the start signal, participants go under their canoe into the air pocket and swim the canoe to the finish line as fast as possible. The first turtle to cross the line wins. Some boat-to-boat contact will probably occur, so remind participants to keep their hands inside.

iStockphoto/Thinkstock

#12: Turtles and Teacups

Craft: Canoes (Games are suitable for two to four participants per boat, ui
   otherwise.)

Skill Level: Any

Water: Calm flatwater, deep enough for participants to stand at shoulder depth or
   deeper

Playing Area: Clear open area, but small enough to easily monitor

Supplies: Canoes

Skills: In-water confidence

Note: Be sure to instruct participants to keep their hands and fingers inside the upside-
   down boat, using the thwarts to push and "drive." This technique will help prevent
   finger injuries if boats collide.

For this game, you will need to establish start and finish lines, and will need something
capable of making a loud noise that can be heard by the participants from under the
canoes. Canoes start in upside-down position, and participants are in the water. Assign
two to four participants per canoe. At the start line, have participants arrange canoes so
that bows are on the start line, facing the direction of the finish line, with at least six feet
between boats.

Explain to the participants that right-side-up boats are teacups and upside-down
boats are turtles. Participants will start the race as turtles (like in #11 Turtle Races).
However, when they hear the signal, they must flip the boat over, climb in, and continue
the race by hand-paddling the canoe full of water, thus becoming the teacup. At the
next signal, they flip the boat back over and race again as turtles, and then again as
teacups, and so forth. Continue alternating as often as you wish (or as much as you
can manage while laughing). The first canoe to cross the line wins. Some boat-to-boat
contact will probably occur, so remind participants to keep their hands inside the boat
when it is upside-down.

5

Games and Activities
for Safety and Rescue

Paul Greggs/Liquid Lessons

Please note that some of the activities found in Chapter 4 are also suitable to be used in conjunction with self-rescue instruction.

#13: Lifejacket Fit for a Friend

Craft: None required
Skill Level: Any
Water: This activity is on land.
Playing Area: Clear open area
Supplies: Lifejackets
Skills: How to select an appropriately fitting lifejacket

For this activity, you will need an assortment of U.S. Coast Guard–approved lifejackets that are in good, usable condition, in appropriate sizes to fit each participant. Place participants in buddy pairs. Each paddler selects a lifejacket that they believe is the correct size, puts the lifejacket on, and makes sure it is properly fastened.

One buddy holds his arms straight up over his head. The other buddy stands behind him and grasps the top of the lifejacket's arm openings and pulls up, trying to pull the lifejacket off. (For safety, caution participants not to lift their buddy off of the ground). The lifejacket should have no excess room above its front, and the lifejacket should not ride up over the face or chin. If the lifejacket slides off or rides up above the face or chin, then it is too large, or not fastened correctly, and should be exchanged for a smaller lifejacket or refastened. Once the first buddy is situated in a properly fitting jacket, repeat the exercise with the second buddy.

#14: Goldilocks and the Three Lifejackets

Craft: None required
Skill Level: Any
Water: This activity is on land.
Playing Area: Clear open area
Supplies: Lifejackets (see game instructions for details)
Skills: How to select an appropriately fitting lifejacket, correctly wearing a lifejacket

In this version of the story, Goldilocks is in search of the lifejacket that is *just* right. You will need an assortment of U.S. Coast Guard–approved lifejackets that are in good, usable condition, in appropriate sizes to fit each participant, and an assortment of lifejackets in sizes that are too small and too large. Try to mix up the sizes to include as much variation as possible, such as adult jackets for youth groups, youth jackets for adult groups, a lifejacket made for an infant, and so forth.

The objective is that Goldilocks has to find a lifejacket that it too big, one that is too small, and one that is just right. This game can be played by individuals, pairs, or small groups of three or four. If a group, they can designate which participant is playing the role of Goldilocks. Mix lifejackets in a big pile, and have participants pick through and find three lifejackets: one that fits properly, one that is too big, and one that is too small. The individual or group has to be prepared to defend their three selections based on a sound reason for selecting the lifejacket, such as reading the manufacturer's label to ensure the life jacket is a proper fit for their size and weight, the type of lifejacket appropriate to the activity, or demonstrating problems with the fit, such as sliding it off over the head and shoulders of the wearer. This activity can be conducted as a relay race, or a non-competitive activity.

To add variation, change the objective so that Goldilocks has to find one lifejacket that is either too big *or* too small, one that is just right, and one that should be discarded. For this version, you will additionally need an assortment of lifejackets which are no longer in good and serviceable condition; the kind that have been (or should be) discarded for various reasons, such as:

- No longer able to read the U.S. Coast Guard–approved label
- Lifejackets that are damaged with any kind of tears, holes, mildew, rot, or are waterlogged
- Lifejackets which are faded (fabric becomes weak from extensive exposure to sunlight)
- Lifejackets with damaged flotation, flotation which has become hard, or has disintegrated
- Lifejackets with broken zippers, missing ties, missing or frayed webbing, missing or broken buckles, and such

Safety Reminder: People supervising activities should be responsible to ensure that lifejackets that are no longer in serviceable condition are properly discarded. If you are retaining these as examples or supplies for future activities and instruction, be sure to have a system in place to keep them out of service so they are not accidentally used by participants.

#15: Boat-Over-Boat Relays

Craft: Tandem or solo canoes and kayaks
Skill Level: All
Water: Calm, flatwater for learning and practicing
Playing Area: Clear open area
Supplies: Boats
Skills: Assisting with rescue of others

This activity consists of timed drills in performing boat-over-boat rescues. Prior to conducting this activity, participants should have instruction in conducting boat-over-boat rescues appropriate for the craft they are paddling and have had an opportunity to practice these skills.

For this game, you will need to establish a start line for the rescue craft, and a line for where the capsized craft will be positioned. Rescue craft arrange boats so that bows are on the start line, facing the direction of the capsized craft, with at least 10 feet between boats. Participants who will be capsizing arrange their boats so that bows are on the line, facing the direction of the rescue craft, with 8 to 10 feet between boats.

At the direction of the instructor, the "victims" capsize their craft. Once all boats have gone over, instructor gives the signal for the rescue craft to go, and timing begins. Rescue craft paddle as fast as possible to the victims and perform the appropriate boat-over-boat rescue. Time ends when victims are back upright in their own boat ready to paddle. Repeat the activity; the objective is improving the time.

Variations:

- Have boats start in the "T" (or "A") formation with the victims already in the water, and time from the "go" signal.
- Position boats close to each other in pairs. Start time from when the "victim" craft flips over to when the victims are back upright in their own boat ready to paddle.
- Add the use of a rescue sling, or "scooping," as part of the rescue.

In the canoe-over-canoe rescue in the standard "T" formation, the overturned boat is brought across the middle (amidships) of the rescue canoe. The rescue craft can be either a solo or tandem canoe. The rescue craft in the "A" formation must be a tandem canoe. For the canoe-over-canoe rescue in the A formation, the overturned canoe is brought to the bow of the rescue boat, at about a 45-degree angle to the gunwale at the bow, thus creating the A. In this rescue, the bow paddler remains in his position, facing forward, and is the only person in the rescue craft who handles the capsized craft. The stern paddler adds direction and stability to the rescue craft by continuing to paddle and bracing if needed. The remainder of the rescue is the same as the T, except that, again, only the bow paddler makes contact with the capsized craft. Rescue using the A formation is often more efficient than using the T formation, as no time is wasted in having paddlers change positions (at either the start of the rescue or when finished), and the stern paddler continues to provide momentum and steering as needed, which helps prevent the loss of contact between boats, or misalignment, that sometimes occurs when using the T.

#16: Help and Huddle

Craft: None required. This game is an in-water swimming activity.
Skill Level: Any
Water: Flatwater, or swimming pool
Playing Area: Clear open area, deeper than where participants can stand
Supplies: Lifejackets
Skills: Self-rescue in cold water when wearing a lifejacket

In this activity, participants practice what they should do if they fall into cold water while wearing a lifejacket, in the event they had to float in the water and wait to be rescued. The intent of both of these positions is to retain body heat while reducing the amount of energy required to keep the body afloat. While wearing lifejackets, have participants enter the water and practice floating in each position.

- *HELP Position*: HELP stands for *Heat Escape Lessening Posture*. To float in the HELP position, pull the knees up to chest, with the arms tucked in close against or across the chest, while keeping the face forward and out of the water. This position is used when a person is alone.
- *Huddle Position*: Use the huddle position when two or more people are in the water. Everyone comes together face-to-face and places their arms over each other's shoulders so that sides are touching, making a circle. Children or small adults can be placed in the middle of the huddle where they will be warmer.

Safety Reminder: These positions are not safe to be used in river currents or whitewater.

#17: Cow Tipping

Craft: Kayaks, canoes
Skill Level: Good boat control, ability to execute boat-over-boat rescue
Water: Flatwater
Playing Area: Large clear open area
Supplies: Boats, paddles
Skills: Connecting strokes and maneuvers, executing rescue
Note: Capsizing and executing rescue is an intentional part of this game.

You will need a minimum of eight boats to play this game, more is preferable. Establish a large playing area with defined boundaries. Designate one boat as "it" (the evil cow tipper), two boats as farmers, and the rest of the paddlers are cows.

In this game, the cow tipper tags a cow by touching the cow's boat with a paddle, and simultaneously giving a loud "Wheeeee-haw!" The cow, now awake but frozen in terror, must stop paddling, moo twice, and flip over. Then, a farmer assists with the appropriate boat-over-boat rescue. Once the cow has been rescued, he becomes a farmer. Cows can be protected from tipping by two farmer boats flanking the cow boat. (However, if a rescue is required, the two farmer boats must leave to attend to the tipped cow). Game play stops when all of the cows are protected, or no more cows are left to tip. *Note:* The game play does not stop during a rescue (unless the instructor needs to specifically stop the game for safety reasons).

#18: Stop, Drop, and Roll

Craft: Kayaks
Skill Level: Good boat control, ability to execute complete kayak rolls in calm water
Water: Flatwater
Playing Area: Large clear open area
Supplies: Boats, paddles
Skills: Connecting strokes and maneuvers, executing rolling as self-rescue
Note: Capsizing and executing rescue is an intentional part of this activity.

For this game, you will need to establish start and finish lines. Kayakers arrange boats so that bows are on the start line, facing the direction of the finish line, with at least 10 feet between boats. At the start signal, paddlers begin racing toward the finish line. At the "Stop, drop, and roll" signal, paddlers stop paddling forward, flip over, and roll back up, then continue paddling forward. Instructor continues calling "Stop, drop, and roll" as desired. The first paddler to cross the finish line wins. (For safety, be sure to establish a second, easily defined signal that will tell paddlers to stop racing, in the event that rescue needs to be conducted or other incident occurs.)

#19: Throw Bag Relay

Craft: None required.
Skill Level: Any
Water: Relay game on land, can be also practiced on water
Playing Area: Clear open area
Supplies: Throw bags
Skills: Learning to throw a throw bag

Prior to conducting this activity, participants should have instruction in how to use and execute rescue using a throw bag, and they should have had an opportunity to practice these skills. For this activity, you will need one throw bag per team. Each bag should contain the same length of rope. Establish a throwing line and a rescue line. The distance between the throwing line and rescue line should be shorter than the length of throw-bag rope in use for the game. Divide participants into even teams.

Teams line up single file behind the throwing line. The first person in the line from each team goes to the rescue line as that team's first victim. At the start signal, the victim pretends to drown, and the team member at the front of the line must throw the bag so that the rope lands within the victim's reach. Victims may take no more than one step in any one direction to retrieve the rope. If the rescuer misses, he has to retrieve the rope, restuff the bag, and throw again. Or, as restuffing the throw bag often takes a great deal of time, you may prefer to have participants simulate filling the bag with water (which is what they would do in the event of a real missed throw) by having them stuff the bag with three or four tennis balls. Once the victim has the rope, he must turn backward, put the rope over his shoulder, and be "pulled" in by the rescuer, simulating the correct stance and hand positions pulling the rope back. Once across the throwing line, the victim assists in the quick restuffing of the throw bag. The person who was the rescuer runs to the other end as the new victim, and the next person in line becomes the rescuer. The last victim goes to the end of the line to wait his turn as the rescuer. The first team to have everyone complete the rescue is the winner.

Increase the challenge by requiring participants to get the rope within reaching distance without the victim being allowed to take the step, or look to improve their times. This activity can be conducted in the water as well.

#20: Rescue Rodeo

Craft: Canoes, kayaks

Skill Level: Participants should have already learned and practiced whatever rescue skills will be included in the rodeo activity.

Water: Flatwater

Playing Area: Large clear open area ·

Supplies: Boats, paddles, rescue equipment required based on the activities selected

Skills: Self-rescue, assisting in rescue

In a regular rodeo, cowboys compete in a series of events, such as barrel racing, steer wrestling, roping, or bull riding. For this rodeo, you will be setting up a series of rescue events. The number and type of activities selected can be as varied as you want, and can be set up based on the number of boats, types of boats, space available, time available, and skill level of participants. Participant teams can do the same event at the same time, or if you have enough supervision to safely monitor the activities, you can run more than one event at a time, with teams rotating from one event to the next. To make it competitive like a real rodeo, each event is timed, and the team with the lowest total score from all events combined wins.

Paul Greggs/Liquid Lessons

Sample Events for Tandem Canoe Rescue Rodeo

- Event #1: Paddlers race from one point to another, change positions, and return to the finish line.
- Event #2: At the start line, paddle out to a designated point, flip the boat over so it fills with water, climb back in, and hand-paddle to the finish line.
- Event #3: Hold Turtle Races (see #11: Turtle Races in Chapter 4).
- Event #4: At the start line, paddle out to a designated point, flip the boat over, participants have to go under the boat and sing a specified song, then perform a Capistrano flip (see Note), re-enter the canoe, and paddle back to the finish line
- Event #5: At the start line, paired boats paddle out to a designated point, where the "victim" craft flips over, paired boats perform a canoe-over-canoe rescue, and after the victims have re-entered their canoe, both boats paddle back to the finish line as team.

Note: The Capistrano flip is currently taught by some, but not all, of the canoeing instructional certification programs. The Capistrano flip is a self-rescue technique for emptying water from a swamped canoe in deep water. It is best performed by two or more paddlers. After the canoe has swamped, it is turned upside down, capturing a large air pocket underneath. Paddlers go underneath, and in unison lift up on one gunwale to break the suction seal, and then *quickly* throw the canoe up and over so that it lands right-side-up, mostly empty of water. Paddlers then re-enter the emptied canoe. For the Capistrano flip to work, paddlers must be coordinated in their timing, and lift up and throw the boat over at the same time. A strong, coordinated scissors kick will help. Breaking the suction seal by lifting up on one gunwale is critical before attempting to raise the canoe out of the water. Ideally, the boat will end up mostly empty; however, even a poorly executed maneuver will remove a good deal of water.

6

Games and Activities for Flatwater

©Don Kohlbauer/San Diego Union-Tribune/ZUMA Press

#21: Duck

Craft: Canoes
Skill Level: Any
Water: Flatwater
Playing Area: Large clear open area
Supplies: Boats, paddles, rubber duck (or ball) per boat
Skills: Steering, turning, connecting strokes and maneuvers, improving communication in tandem craft

Establish a playing area with defined boundaries. The size will depend on how many boats are playing, as well as the paddling skill of participants. Make the area smaller for novice boaters, and larger for experienced paddlers.

Each boat starts with one rubber duck. In this tag game, every canoe is "it" at the same time. The object is to toss the duck into another canoe, while at the same time avoiding having anyone toss a duck into his canoe. The ideal is to remain "duck-free." In order to get rid of a duck, paddlers must throw or place it in another canoe, and yell, "Duck!" If it lands in the water, the duck still "belongs" to the throwing boat, and must be retrieved by them. This game allows no "tag-backs" ("duck-backs"); a duck that lands in a boat cannot be thrown back into the canoe from which it was thrown. Paddles may not be used as bats to deflect ducks, other boats, or other paddlers.

#22: Go to Whoa

Craft: Kayaks, canoes
Skill Level: Ability to execute fundamental forward and steering strokes, and to stop craft when in forward motion
Water: Flatwater
Playing Area: Clear open area
Supplies: Boats, paddles, buoys
Skills: Starting the boat from a standstill, building momentum, stopping in control, improving paddling technique, improving communication for tandem boaters

The object of this activity is to go from a standstill, paddle as quickly as possible to the stop point, and come to a dead stop, without going past the stop line in and doing so shortest amount of time.

Using buoys, set out a course with start and stop points. Note that the stop point has to be clearly defined. Boats start on the start line, and proceed as quickly as possible to the stop line, where they must quickly come to a stop without passing the stop point end line. Each boat works to improve its time getting from the start to the finish. You can allot penalties for not stopping within the stop box.

#23: Red Light, Green Light

Craft: Kayaks, canoes

Skill Level: Ability to execute fundamental forward and steering strokes, and ability to stop the craft when in forward motion

Water: Flatwater

Playing Area: Clear open area

Supplies: Boats, paddles

Skills: Stopping in control, improving paddling technique, improving communication for tandem boaters

The object of this activity is to come to a dead stop as quickly as possible. Have participants arrange boats so that bows are on the start line, facing the direction of the finish line, with about four to six feet between boats. The caller is on the finish line. When the caller says, "Green light," players paddle as fast as they can toward the finish line. When the caller says, "Red light," they must come to a sudden and complete stop. Boats not stopped in time go back to the start line. The first boat that crosses the finish line wins.

As bringing boats to a sudden stop can be challenging, especially for novice paddlers, the caller can give players a set time after saying "Red light" to have their boats at standstill, such as counting down, "Red light, five, four, three, two, one." Increase the count down if paddlers are struggling; reduce the stop time as skills increase.

#24: Sky Writing

Craft: Kayaks, canoes

Skill Level: Good boat control, including ability to execute various turning strokes

Water: Flatwater

Playing Area: Large clear open area

Supplies: Boats, paddles

Skills: Steering, turning, connecting strokes and maneuvers, controlled paddling and precision, improving communication in tandem craft

Just as if a plane were to write something in the sky that can be read from the ground, paddlers are challenged to "write" using their boat, so that a plane passing overhead could see and read it on the water. Give everyone the same word to write out, or have them write the first name of the bow paddler, or something of that sort. Emphasize that their writing must be clear and neat, as precision is important in being able to read what they write. Modify the challenge by selecting either cursive or block letter writing.

#25: Paddle Grip Flip

Craft: Kayaks
Skill Level: Any
Water: Flatwater
Playing Area: Clear open area
Supplies: Kayaks, kayak paddles
Skills: Paddle hand position, relationship of where paddle strokes occur and effect on the boat

Paddlers are going to be using five different paddle grips during this activity:
- *Way Wide:* Kayak paddle in front, hands as far apart as possible, almost touching the blades.
- *Touch Together:* Kayak paddle in front, hands centered and touching.
- *Crisscross Front:* Kayak paddle in front, crisscross hands, with a space in between.
- *Back Grip:* Kayak paddle behind back, hands shoulder-distance apart, knuckles facing forward.
- *Crisscross Back:* Kayak paddle behind back, crisscross arms, knuckles facing forward.

For this game, you will need to establish two end lines. The distance between ends will depend on the skills of the paddlers, numbers of boats, and time available. (To make it more interesting, you can also set this up as an obstacle course.) Have participants arrange boats so that bows are on the start line, facing the direction of the finish line, with about 10 feet between boats.

The object is for participants to paddle from end line to end line, using a different paddle grip each lap. Decide if they will change to a new grip at each end, or have them paddle down and back, and then switch to the next paddle grip. (*Hint:* If having paddlers change to a new grip at each end, have them complete the first five laps with the modified grips, and then paddle normally for the last lap, which will bring them back to the start point.)

Safety Reminder: Note that some of the various paddle positions may cause a participant's arm or shoulder to move out of the paddler's box, which could result in injury. Be sure the on-water playing area is clear of any rocks or other hard objects that could cause shoulder dislocation if tagged by a paddle blade during play.

#26: Blindfold Trust Paddle

Craft: Tandem kayaks, tandem canoes
Skill Level: Good boat control, including ability to execute various turning strokes
Water: Flatwater
Playing Area: Large clear open area
Supplies: Boats, paddles, blindfolds (one per boat)
Skills: Connecting strokes and maneuvers, improving communication

Set up an on-water obstacle course, using buoys or other markers. Bow paddlers are blindfolded, and then the boats navigate the obstacle course. The boats should start one at a time, spaced out so that the conversation between paddlers in one boat doesn't interrupt paddlers in another boat. Once the paddlers have completed the obstacle course, it's a good idea to debrief and talk about what went well, or not so well. Then, do the course a second time with the stern paddler wearing the blindfold this time. Add more challenge by timing them and having them work to decrease their time.

#27: Synchronized Paddling

Craft: Canoes, kayaks
Skill Level: Any
Water: Flatwater
Playing Area: Large clear open area
Supplies: Boats, paddles
Skills: Connecting strokes and maneuvers, stroke precision, improving communication for tandem boats

Boats are spaced far enough apart that they won't come in contact when turning, side slipping, and the like. Boats start with bows facing the instructor. The instructor gives direction as to what he wants the paddlers to do, and all boats perform the task at the same time. Examples: Spin to the boat's onside five times, paddle straight backward 20 strokes, side-slip left, and such. Instructors can give direction as to specific strokes they want to see used, and also can have paddlers connect specific maneuvers, such as performing figure eights, U-turns, and the like. This activity is good for observing participants, as you can see which paddlers have mastered which strokes. All strokes and maneuvers can be practiced with this activity.

#28: Clothespin Tag

Craft: Kayaks, canoes
Skill Level: Good boat control, including ability to execute various turning strokes
Water: Flatwater
Playing Area: Large clear open area
Supplies: Boats, paddles, three spring–style clothespins per paddler (plus lots of extras for loss/breakage)
Skills: Connecting strokes and maneuvers, using what they know to make the boat go
Note: Capsizing is common and should be planned for.

Establish a playing area with defined boundaries. The size will depend on how many boats are playing, as well as the paddling skill of participants. Make the area smaller for novice boaters, and the larger area for experienced paddlers. Be sure you are using the type of clothespins with the spring. Have each paddler clip the three clothespins to the shoulder of the lifejacket (where the armhole rests on the shoulder.) All clothespins don't have to be on the same shoulder.

This activity is another tag game where everyone is "it" at the same time. The object is to retain all three of your own original clothespins, while taking as many as possible from others.

Game Rules:

- May only take one clothespin at a time from another paddler.
- In order to take another clothespin from a player from whom you already took one, you must first take a clothespin from someone else, and then you may return to a previous victim.
- Clothespins that you take from someone else go in the bottom of the boat; they do not get clipped on to your lifejacket.
- Clothespins that are in the bottom of the boat may not be taken by others; only those clothespins that are clipped on to the lifejacket are fair game for taking.
- Participants who have lost all three of their clothespins can continue to play; no one is ever "out."

Scoring: Count up the total from the bottom of the boat, and what is left on any lifejackets. Score as follows:
- Original clothespins retained on the lifejacket: 3 points each
- Stolen clothespins: 1 point each

For tandem boats, you can modify by making this contest a team effort and total the points by boat, or pair up boats to make teams.

#29: Duck, Duck, Goose

Craft: Canoes, kayaks

Skill Level: Good boat control, including ability to execute various tuı
ability to paddle backward

Water: Flatwater

Playing Area: Large clear open area

Supplies: Boats, paddles

Skills: Steering, turning, paddling backward, reacting to execute correct strokes and maneuvers

Note: Be aware of boat collisions, especially if canoes and kayaks are mixed together.

A paddling version of the traditional children's game. Set up by arranging the boats in a "pinwheel" formation, with either bows or sterns in the center. Select one boat as "it," who starts on the outside and paddles a circle around the other boats, tapping each boat as it passes by. That boat makes the rounds, saying, "Duck," until reaching the boat they want to tag, at which point they say, "Goose," and the chase is on. The object is to be the first boat back in the space vacated by the goose. The boat left out becomes the new "it."

The key to making this game work is to ensure everyone has a fair chance. If some participants are paddling very maneuverable boats and others are not, or if the paddling skill levels vary greatly, you may need to add some elements that "slow down" the naturally faster craft. Having boats change direction is one way to make play fair. You may also opt to have the "it" boat perform a certain task, such as sing a short song, before they resume paddling.

Example 1: Sterns in the center of the pinwheel, bows facing out. When tagged, the goose paddles out forward and continues paddling forward around the circle, trying to beat the "it" boat back to the space. The "it" boat stops when it tags the goose, and then has to paddle backward around the circle to try to beat the goose boat back to the space.

Example 2: Bows in the center of the pinwheel, sterns facing out. When tagged, the goose paddles out backward and then paddles forward around the circle, trying to beat the "it" boat back to the space. The "it" boat stops when it tags the goose, and then has to paddle backward around the circle to try to beat the goose boat back to the space.

#30: Dead Fish Polo

Craft: Canoes, kayaks

Skill Level: Good boat control, including ability to execute various turning strokes

Water: Flatwater

Playing Area: Large clear open area

Supplies: Boats, paddles, large-size foam ball or sponge, four buoys for goals, whistle for the referee

Skills: Steering, turning, reacting to execute correct strokes and maneuvers

Note: Capsizing and boat collisions are common. If a boat capsizes during play, stop play, execute rescue, and then resume play from where everyone was.

You will need a minimum of eight boats to play this game; more boats are preferable. Establish a large, rectangular-shaped playing area with defined boundaries. Set two buoys at each end for goals. The goal buoys should be about three to four feet apart, no farther apart than the length of the shortest boat participating. Divide the group into two teams.

Dead Fish Polo is a passing game, with similarities to both polo and football, and requires a lot of teamwork and strategy. Game play starts with both teams behind the end zone of the goal they are defending. The referee starts play by throwing the dead fish (sponge or sponge ball) into the air in the center of the playing "field," at which point the boats may proceed forward. Whichever boat gets to the dead fish first has possession.

When a participant has possession of the dead fish, they must *immediately* stop paddling. If he is in a tandem boat, both paddlers must stop paddling. Only those players *without* the fish in their boat may paddle. To move the fish down the field, participants hand or throw it to their teammates. To score a goal, the boat with the fish in it has to pass between the buoys at the goal line, and go all the way through, either bow to stern, or stern to bow. Of course, this aspect is tricky because the paddler(s) of this boat cannot be paddling, since they are in possession of the fish. Goal tending is permitted.

Establish firm safety rules before playing. Remind players that paddles may not be used as bats to deflect the dead fish, other boats, or other paddlers. Be aware that collisions between boaters during this game are often intentional, as one paddler tries to "take out" a competitor by pushing him out of the way or by capsizing the boat. Determine boat-ramming rules, including penalties as needed, based on the competitive nature of the group. Helmets must be worn by kayakers, and may be a good idea for everyone.

#31: Freeze Tag

Craft: Canoes, kayaks
Skill Level: Any
Water: Flatwater
Playing Area: Large clear open area
Supplies: Boats, paddles
Skills: Steering, turning, connecting, and executing strokes and maneuvers

Establish a playing area with defined boundaries. The size will depend on how many boats are playing, as well as the paddling skill of participants. Make the area smaller for novice boaters, larger for experienced paddlers.

Select one boat as "it" (more if the group is large). Tagging a boat occurs by "it" touching another boat with their paddle. Once tagged, the participant(s) must stop paddling, and place their paddle(s) in or on the boat. A frozen player may become unfrozen by being tagged by another free player, and then may resume playing. Game play ends when everyone is frozen.

#32: One-of-Each-ie

Craft: Canoes, kayaks
Skill Level: Any
Water: Flatwater
Playing Area: Large clear open area
Supplies: Boats, paddles, assorted objects that will float
Skills: Steering, turning, connecting, and executing strokes and maneuvers

For this game, you will need five to seven discernibly different floatable objects, and enough of each different object for one per boat playing. (For example, if you have 10 boats participating, you will need 10 rubber ducks, 10 yellow balls, 10 white balls, 10 orange sponges, and so forth.) Participants must be able to tell the difference between objects, such as by color or shape. Establish a start point and end point. The set-up is to distribute each different object in various locations around your paddling area.

The object of the game is for each boat to collect one of each item (one-of-each-ie), which are floating about in various locations of the paddling area, and be the first to return to finish line or location with the items. In addition to having the participants retrieve the objects, you can include paddlers having to change positions, getting out on the beach to retrieve an object on land, sing a song, and such, as well.

#33: Protector Tag

Craft: Canoes (Kayaks can play if soft balls are used and participants are tagged like in dodgeball.)
Skill Level: Any
Water: Flatwater
Playing Area: Large clear open area
Supplies: Boats, paddles, balls
Skills: Connecting and executing strokes and maneuvers

Select one boat as the movie star, who must be protected from the paparazzi at all times. Select two or three boats to be the bodyguards (increase the number, depending on the size of the group). The rest of the boats are paparazzi, and are each issued a ball or other throwable. The object for the paparazzi is to throw their ball in to the movie star's boat. The object for the bodyguards is to keep this from happening. This game starts more or less with a circle, with the movie star in the center, the bodyguards positioned around to protect them, and the paparazzi in an outer ring. This game will travel and change shapes as the paparazzi try to outmaneuver the bodyguards. The movie star is also paddling, and so is able to help in their self-protection. (A variation is to not allow the movie star to paddle.)

- A ball is thrown into the movie star's boat by paparazzi = Paparazzi and movie star trade places.
- A ball thrown by paparazzi is caught by a bodyguard = Paparazzi trades places with bodyguard.
- A ball thrown by paparazzi lands in the bodyguard's boat = Bodyguard trades places with paparazzi.

You can make this game even more challenging by adding other scoring or consequences, such as having to spin the boat three times clockwise when tagged, sing a song, and so forth. The characters in this game can be modified to better suit the clientele you are serving, such as president, CIA, and terrorists.

#34: Marching Band

Craft: Canoes, kayaks
Skill Level: Any
Water: Flatwater
Playing Area: Large clear open area
Supplies: Boats, paddles
Skills: Connecting and improving strokes and maneuvers, stroke precision, improving communication for tandem boats

This game is a synchronized paddling activity that requires precision, and includes the group working together to synchronize maneuvers, rather than individual boats performing the tasks at their own pace. The object of this activity is to perform maneuvers as a group with the precision of a competitive marching band on the football field. When band members are marching on the field, they must maintain perfectly straight lines when marching forward, backward, and sideways. Various strokes and maneuvers can be practiced with this activity. Just like band members, in this activity, paddlers must perform the maneuvers while keeping the tips of the bows on every boat in perfect alignment. Boats line up side-by-side, with just enough distance between them to allow for paddling, bow tips aligned.

Assign the following tasks to the paddlers:
- Paddle a set distance forward.
- Paddle a set distance backward.
- Paddle a set distance sideways, then repeat the other direction.

To help paddlers progress to accomplishing this goal as a group, you may want to start by having a pair of boats accomplish the tasks, then go to four boats in a group, gradually increasing to the whole class.

To add a visual element so that participants can better see the line as they practice, string some brightly colored plastic surveyor's tape or caution tape along the bow tips, attached to the two end boats. Both types of tape are made of thin plastic, which breaks easily, and so it will not be a hazard in the event of capsize. For safety, do not tie boats together with rope, twine, or anything else that won't break away easily in the event of capsize.

#35: Obstacle Course

Craft: Canoes, kayaks
Skill Level: Any
Water: Flatwater
Playing Area: Large clear open area
Supplies: Boats, paddles, buoys (or other markers)
Skills: Connecting and improving strokes and maneuvers, improving communication for tandem boats

The object of this activity is to complete going through an obstacle course. Time participants through the course, and then work on skills to improve their times. The set-up can be as simple or complex as desired. In addition to buoys, utilize bridges, pilings, docks, and such when possible. In addition to going around, under, and through obstacles, you can add challenge by having participants complete certain maneuvers, such has having to spin the boat a set number of times at a location, or change positions. Various strokes and maneuvers can be practiced with this activity.

#36: Follow the Leader

Craft: Canoes, kayaks
Skill Level: Any
Water: Flatwater
Playing Area: Large clear open area
Supplies: Boats, paddles
Skills: Executing strokes and maneuvers

Select one boat as the leader. The other paddlers line up single file behind the leader, leaving a boat's length between them. The lead boat paddles whatever course they want to set, and the followers must execute the same. When giving instruction, encourage participants to vary their maneuvers as much as possible when it is their turn as the leader, such as paddling backward, executing turns, spins, side-slipping, and such. Various strokes and maneuvers can be practiced with this activity. Switch out who gets to be the leader after a certain amount of time, or after a set distance.

#37: Rabbits and Hunters

Craft: Canoes, kayaks
Skill Level: Good boat control
Water: Flatwater
Playing Area: Large clear open area
Supplies: Boats, paddles, one large foam ball or sponge
Skills: Reacting to execute correct strokes and maneuvers, starting and stopping, boat control, teamwork

Establish a playing area with defined boundaries. The size will depend on how many boats are playing, as well as the paddling skill of participants. Make the area smaller for novice boaters, larger for experienced paddlers. Designate one boat as the "hunter," and the remaining boats are "rabbits." The hunters use the ball to shoot (tag) the rabbits.

- Hunters tag rabbits by hitting them with the ball. Head shots don't count.
- The hunter boat may paddle while in possession of the ball; however, in order to shoot, *they must come to a complete stop before throwing the ball.* They cannot throw while the boat is still in motion.
- Once a rabbit is tagged, he becomes a hunter (tandem boats play as a team, so if one of the tandem boats is tagged, they both become hunters).
- Hunters may pass the ball to other hunters.
- Only one ball is in play to use to shoot the rabbits.

The game ends once no more rabbits remain. The last rabbit tagged becomes the first hunter in the next round of play. To add more challenge (and chaos), have more than one ball in play for the hunters.

#38: Frozen Duck Relay

Craft: Kayaks
Skill Level: Any
Water: Flatwater
Playing Area: Large clear open area
Supplies: Boats, paddles, rubber ducks (one per paddler), buoys (or other markers)
Skills: Connecting and improving strokes and maneuvers, balance

Establish a playing area, including start and finish lines. Maintain a good distance between the start and end. Have participants arrange boats so that bows are on the start line, facing the direction of the finish line, with about four to six feet between boats.

The goal of this game is to get the entire group from the start line to the finish line. At the start, paddlers line up, balance a rubber duck on their head, and then proceed to paddle toward the finish line. However, if a rubber duck falls off of a paddler's head, that paddler is frozen and must stop paddling and wait for assistance. The only way to get unfrozen is for another paddler to pick up his duck and place it back on his head. However, if the duck falls off while helping, the helper, too, is frozen until someone else comes to help them as well. The game ends when everyone is either frozen or has gotten to the finish line. If everyone becomes frozen, allow some time for the group to discuss strategy, and then restart the game.

As the group progresses to being able to get everyone from one side to another, increase the challenge by timing how long it takes for them to complete the game, and then have them work to improve their time. You can also add more challenge by increasing the distance between the start and end lines. Various strokes and maneuvers can be practiced with this activity.

#39: Progression Tag

Craft: Canoes
Skill Level: Any
Water: Flatwater
Playing Area: Large clear open area
Supplies: Boats, paddles, ball (or other soft throwable)
Skills: Steering, turning, connecting strokes and maneuvers

Establish a playing area with defined boundaries. The size will depend on how many boats are playing, as well as the paddling skill of participants. Make the area smaller for novice boaters, and larger for experienced paddlers.

Select one boat as "it," which starts with the ball. Tagging a boat occurs by "it" throwing or placing the ball into another canoe. Once tagged, the canoe with the ball in it also becomes an "it," and works with the first boat to tag the next boat. Each boat that is tagged becomes part of the "it." The last boat left untagged wins and becomes the new "it" for the next round of play.

#40: Pass Tag

Craft: Canoes, kayaks
Skill Level: Good boat control
Water: Flatwater
Playing Area: Large clear open area
Supplies: Boats, paddles, buoys, balls (or other throwables)
Skills: Steering, turning, reacting to execute correct strokes and maneuvers

Establish a large playing area with defined boundaries. Select two or more participants to be "it" (more depending on the number of players). Set out half as many balls as participating boats. The object of this game is for the "not it" players to work together to help everyone remain untagged.

- If a participant (or tandem boat) being chased is holding a ball, he cannot be tagged.
- When a participant (or tandem boat) has possession of a ball, he cannot paddle.
- The ball may not be passed back and forth between two boats. It must be passed to a third boat before it can return back.
- Tagging occurs by "it" touching another boat with the hand.

#41: Aliens, Cows, and Farmers

Craft: Canoes, kayaks
Skill Level: Good boat control
Water: Flatwater
Playing Area: Large clear open area
Supplies: Boats, paddles, buoys
Skills: Steering, turning, reacting to execute correct strokes and maneuvers

You will need a minimum of eight boats to play this game; more boats are preferable. Establish a large, rectangular-shaped playing area with defined boundaries. Set buoys at each end to mark end lines, and another buoy should be set in the center of the playing area.

Before playing, participants need to know three signs:
- *The Sign of the Alien*: Place both hands behind your head, pointing fingers up to make antennae, while saying, "Wheedle, wheedle, wheedle" in a high-pitched voice.
- *The Sign of the Cow*: Place both hands in front of you in fist shape, with thumbs at the top and pinky fingers at the bottom, knuckles forward. Alternative hands going up and down, as if milking a cow, while quickly saying, "Moo, moo, moo, moo"
- *The Sign of the Farmer*: Hold paddle overhead and wave it about while saying, "Hey, you aliens, get away from my cows!"

Have the group practice making the signs. Next, explain the following: Aliens chase cows, cows chase farmers, and farmers chase aliens.

Divide the group into two teams. For each round of play, each team is given a short time to huddle and decide which sign to show, and then both teams line up at the center line, facing each other to start the game. At the whistle, each side shows their selected sign. Whichever team shows the stronger sign becomes "it"—the chasers. The other team, with the "weaker" sign, is being chased. (This tag game is similar to Rock, Paper, Scissors.) For example, if one team shows the alien sign, and the other team shows the cow sign, the aliens are then "it" and are chasing the team that showed the cow sign. If both teams show the same sign, it's a tie, and they must immediately show a second sign.

The goal is for each team to gain members from the other team. Those players being chased have to make it past the end line they were facing at the start to be safe. If they are tagged, they become part of the other team. Tagging occurs by touching another boat with one's hand. The round of play ends when everyone is either tagged or safe, and then another round of play starts at the center line again.

#42: Ships to Sea

Craft: Canoes, kayaks
Skill Level: Good boat control
Water: Flatwater
Playing Area: Large clear open area
Supplies: Boats, paddles, buoys, water gun (or spray bottle)
Skills: Steering, turning, and reacting to execute correct strokes and maneuvers

Ships to Sea is a great game for a hot day. Establish a large playing area (sea) with defined boundaries. Set buoys at each end to mark "safe zones" (ports). Select one or more participants to be "it" (whales), and give them a water gun or spray bottle, which they will use to spout water. Divide the rest of the boats (ships) into two even groups, sending each to a different end of the playing area.

The object of the game is for the ships to cross the sea without getting sprayed (tagged) by the whale's waterspout. Ships start in the ports, which are safe zones. Whales are in the sea between the ports, and may not cross the line into the ports. The whale(s) calls out, "All ships to sea," at which time all ships must leave the safety of the ports and cross the sea as quickly as possible to the other ports. The whales try to "tag" the players by spraying them with water. Those players who are sprayed (tagged) become icebergs floating around in the sea. They don't paddle; rather, they simply float about, creating blocks to passage. Those players who cross safely into the port are safe until the whales call, "All ships to sea," and the game play starts again. The last boat left is the winner and becomes the next "it" in the new round of play.

Paul Greggs/Liquid Lessons

#43: Batty Baseball

Craft: Canoes, kayaks
Skill Level: Good boat control
Water: Flatwater
Playing Area: Large clear open area
Supplies: Boats, paddles, buoys, plastic ball
Skills: Steering, turning, reacting to execute correct strokes and maneuvers

This game requires a minimum of 10 boats to play; more boats are better. Set up the playing area as you would set up a baseball field, with four buoys as bases. Divide the group into two. One team will be up at bat first; the other team is the outfield and pitcher. (For some groups it may be best to have the instructor pitch.) When playing with tandem boats, the bow paddler bats, and then partners switch positions for the next time up at bat. In this game, participant's paddles are used as the bat. The batter stays at bat until they get a hit. When they get a hit, they paddle ("run") around the bases. The "runner" must touch the base with their paddle, rather than go overtop of it. After the ball has been fielded by one player, it must be thrown around the field to every boat on the fielding team until everyone has touched the ball. When the last fielder touches the ball, they yell "stop" at which point the "runner" must stop where they are and not start" running" again until the next player hits the ball. There are no tag outs at bases. Teams switch sides after a pre-determined number of players have run the bases, or after everyone on the batting team has been up to bat.

#44: Elbow Tag

Craft: Kayaks
Skill Level: Good boat control
Water: Flatwater
Playing Area: Large clear open area
Supplies: Kayaks, buoys
Skills: Steering, turning, reacting to execute correct strokes and maneuvers

Establish a playing area with defined boundaries. The size will depend on how many boats are playing, as well as the paddling skill of participants. Make the area smaller for novice boaters, larger for experienced paddlers. Participants are hand-paddling for this activity.

For this game, you will need an odd number of players who are "not it," so select the number of players who are "it" to make this number come out correctly. The not-it boaters scatter throughout the playing area. At the start signal, "it" tries to tag the other boats by touching the boat with his hand. In order to be safe from being tagged, two paddlers partner up by hooking elbows. As long as they are connected, they cannot be tagged. However, at any time another paddler being chased by an "it" can come up on the free side of either paddler and connect. When this happens, the other partner must break free and paddle away, becoming one who is being chased, and trying to connect elbows with a new partner.

#45: Vampire Tag*

Craft: Canoes, kayaks
Skill Level: Good boat control
Water: Flatwater
Playing Area: Large clear open area
Supplies: Boats, paddles
Skills: Steering, turning, reacting to execute correct strokes and maneuvers

Vampire Tag is a great large-group game, with lots of chaos and fun. You will need a minimum of 10 boats to play this game; more boats are preferable. Establish a playing area with defined boundaries. The size will depend on how many boats are playing, as well as the paddling skill of participants. Make the area smaller for novice boaters, or larger for experienced paddlers.

This activity is a tag game, where who is "it" and who is being chased changes based on if it's "daytime" or "nighttime." The game master can change the game from day to night as often as he wants. The more often the game play changes between day and night, the more chaotic the game becomes. Tagging is by touching a boat with a hand.

Designate the boats as follows. Two boats will be the vampire hunters. Divide the remaining boats into two groups: vampires and humans. If you have an odd number, have the extra boat be vampire. The instructor plays as the game master, and will determine if it is daytime or nighttime.

When it's nighttime:
- The vampires come out of their coffins and try to bite (tag) the humans
- Any humans who are bitten (tagged) by vampires become frozen and have to stop paddling.
- The vampire hunters are trying to tag the vampires. Any vampire tagged by the vampire hunter is saved from their fate as a vampire and becomes human
- Any vampires who were tagged by humans in the daytime are frozen until being unfrozen by another vampire tagging them. However, if a frozen vampire is unfrozen by the vampire hunter, he becomes human.

When it's daytime:
- The humans are hunting the vampires.
- Any vampires who are tagged by humans become frozen and have to stop paddling.

*Contributed by David Tyrrell

- The vampire hunters are trying to save the humans. Any humans who were tagged by vampires in the nighttime remain frozen until a vampire hunter tags them. If they are tagged by a vampire hunter, they become unfrozen and remain human. However, if they are not tagged by a vampire hunter before it becomes night again, they become vampires.
- As the vampires are trying to increase their numbers, they are carefully guarding their victims from last night to prevent the vampire hunters from saving them, and can use their boats to block the vampire hunters from tagging the frozen humans.
- Vampire hunters cannot tag vampires in the daytime; however, humans can.

To help keep track of who is who, frozen vampires must cross their arms high across their chests as if they were in their coffins. Frozen humans keep their arms down at their sides. Because of the on-going role changes, the game master may need to pause game play by calling "dusk" at which point everyone reveals what they are at that point in time and can regroup before resuming play. A simplified variation of this game is to have vampires tagging humans when its night, and then switch to humans tagging vampires in the daytime. Start with even sides, and each group works to increase their numbers.

Photo Courtesy of The U.S. Coast Guard

#46: Traffic Cop

Craft: Canoes, kayaks
Skill Level: Good, straightforward paddling skills, working to execute turning maneuvers
Water: Flatwater
Playing Area: Large clear open area
Supplies: Boats, paddles
Skills: Steering, turning, reacting to execute correct strokes and maneuvers

This activity can be used for all levels of skills, from basic steering through more complex turning maneuvers, including transitioning to moving water. In this activity, paddlers are working to increase their reaction time to execute turns.

Set up in a large, open area, with the instructor positioned either in a boat or on a stationary object, such as a dock. Prior to starting, explain the directional signals that will be used. A suggested method is to hold a paddle vertically, paddle end up. When the paddle is straight up and down, it's neutral. Then, when you want the participants to execute their turn, tilt the paddle to point towards the direction you want them to go.

All boats start at a distance away from the instructor, so they are able to gain good forward momentum. Boats go one at a time (to keep things flowing, have a first, second, third order, with a boat on deck ready to go as soon as the boat ahead of it completes its turn). On their turn, participants paddle straight toward the instructor "traffic cop," awaiting the directional signal. The instructor will either point left or right, depending on which way they want the boat to turn, and participants execute appropriate turning strokes. After making their turn, they return to the start point and get in the line of boats to wait for their next turn. (If you have multiple instructors, you can set "traffic cops" in multiple locations and do the drill as a continuous loop.) As skills improve, gradually decrease the distance and time the paddlers have to react and make the turn.

#47: Yo-Yo

Craft: Canoes, kayaks
Skill Level: Ability to execute spins
Water: Flatwater
Playing Area: Large clear open area
Supplies: Boats, paddles
Skills: Executing spins, using momentum, improving synchronized paddling, precision, improving communication in tandem craft

When playing with a yo-yo, you have the dynamic motion required for the yo-yo to go down or up, as well as that moment where the yo-yo is just sort of hanging there at the bottom, spinning, waiting to use the momentum to return to the top. This activity helps paddlers learn to work with both the dynamic motion (the paddle strokes moving the boat through the water) as well as to efficiently use the momentum, or "glide," between strokes.

Have boats space themselves far enough apart so as to not bump into each other while paddling. Give instruction for any specific direction you want for the spin (onside, offside) and which strokes you want performed. The object is for participants to execute spins by using as few strokes as possible.

Have participants count strokes and try to reduce them by riding through the momentum (sometimes called "ride the glide"). To help with synchronizing the stroke timing as well as allowing for the glide, participants can say a slow "Yo" until they need to begin their next stroke, just before the spin tapers off. Note that some participants may see this activity as a "speed" drill and try to rush through the strokes to keep up the speed of the spin. If this result occurs, remind participants that this drill is about precision, finesse, and timing. Having them say the long "Yo" in each spin will also help slow things down, as it serves as a verbal reminder of the objective.

#48: Train Track

Craft: Canoes, kayaks
Skill Level: Ability to paddle straight forward and straight backward
Water: Flatwater
Playing Area: Large clear open area
Supplies: Boats, paddles
Skills: Steering, paddling forward, backward, precision, improving communication in tandem craft

The object of this activity is to paddle a straight line forward and backward, keeping the "train on the track" between two points. Paddlers should spread out so they don't collide. Each boat selects two stationary objects to paddle between, such as a tree on one side of the pond, and a bush on the other. No obstructions should be found between the two points. They connect an imaginary train track between the two points. Starting at the one end, they paddle straight toward the one point, maintaining a straight path, "staying on the track." When they reach the other end, they stop and reverse, paddling backward to the other side, maintaining the same straight path between the two points. As paddlers gain proficiency and improve precision, they can work to increase their speed or try to reduce the number of strokes it takes to get from one side to the other.

#49: Mirror, Mirror

Craft: Tandem canoes
Skill Level: Any
Water: Flatwater
Playing Area: Large clear open area
Supplies: Boats, paddles
Skills: Correcting strokes and maneuvers, improving precision, assessment, and correction

Bow paddlers turn around to face the stern paddlers. Stern paddler in each boat paddles first. The instructor gives direction for what stroke(s) and/or maneuver(s) should be performed. The stern paddler executes while the bow paddler observes. Then, staying where they are, the paddler in the bow does the same strokes; however, he tries to mirror the strokes, doing them in the same manner as they were executed by the stern paddler. The stern paddler observes. The bow paddler offers constructive assistance to help the stern paddler improve upon what was just executed. The stern paddler paddles the same drill again, and they work together to assess and correct. Then, they switch roles (they do not switch ends in the boat) and repeat the exercise.

#50: Dodgeball Tag

Craft: Canoes, kayaks
Skill Level: Good boat control
Water: Flatwater
Playing Area: Large clear open area
Supplies: Boats, paddles, large foam ball (or large sponge)
Skills: Reacting to execute correct strokes and maneuvers

This activity is a combination of dodgeball and tag. Establish a playing area with defined boundaries. The size will depend on how many boats are playing, however for this game to work you will need to keep the area reasonably confined.

- "It" tags players by hitting them with the ball.
- Head shots don't count.
- The "it" cannot paddle while in possession of the ball (for tandem craft, neither partner may paddle while the ball is in the boat).
- The "it" can paddle after throwing the ball to retrieve it, but must stop once the ball is touched, or at the point it is caught by another player.
- If hit, the paddler becomes frozen and must stop paddling (including hand-paddling), but he is not out of the game.
- If a frozen paddler (boat) intercepts the ball, he is unfrozen and comes back into play.
- If the ball is caught by a non-frozen paddler, the "it" boat becomes frozen for a count of 30, and all frozen paddlers/boats become unfrozen.

Photo Courtesy of The U.S. Coast Guard

#51: Twister Tag

Craft: Canoes, kayaks

Skill Level: Good boat control

Water: Flatwater

Playing Area: Large clear open area

Supplies: Boats, paddles, throwables in two different colors, enough for three of each for each paddler

Skills: Reacting to execute correct strokes and maneuvers, spinning

Establish a long rectangular-shaped playing area with defined boundaries. Set two buoys at each end, which are safe zones. Divide the group into two teams. Each team is assigned a color, and each player is given three of the throwables in that color. For example, each player on team A has three orange sponges, and each player on team B has three yellow balls. (If you don't have enough of the same item, mix items keeping the same color, such as yellow balls and yellow sponges. Or, give each team two colors, so team A may have blue sponges and green balls, and team B has yellow sponges, and orange balls.) To help keep track of who is on what team, have participants use same-colored blindfolds as headbands, or loop them through the shoulder of their lifejackets.

The object is to be the first team to move all of their players across the playing area to the safe zone at the opposite end. Each team goes to an opposite end of the playing area and lines up behind the buoys, which mark the end zones. At the start, players paddle forward, trying to get to the other side. As players pass each other, they throw their objects at the other team's players to tag them.

- A tag is either by hitting them with the ball (head shots don't count), or by having the object land in the boat.
- When a player is tagged, he must stop and spin the boat in place three full rotations around, and then he may continue trying to make it to the other end.
- Boats cannot be tagged while spinning.
- Objects thrown may be retrieved and reused.
- Players may only collect the objects of their team's color, and objects which land in boats must be thrown back into the playing area (they cannot be hoarded or thrown into the bushes by the opposing team members).

#52: Hoop Hurl

Craft: Canoes, kayaks

Skill Level: Ability to paddle and steer while paddling backwards

Water: Flatwater

Playing Area: Large clear open area

Supplies: Boats, paddles, hoops (inner tubes, ring buoys, or child's inflatable swim rings will also work), throwables

Skills: reacting to execute correct strokes and maneuvers

The object of this game is for each boat to get rid of their objects first by placing, or hurling, them into the middle of floating hoops, while paddling backward. Set out hoops on the water in various locations so that they are floating throughout the playing area. The farther apart the hoops, the greater distance participants have to paddle between them. Give each paddler/boat the same number of objects as hoops, so that each has one per floating hoop. Establish a start and finish line. At the start, paddlers must travel backward from hoop to hoop, placing one of their objects in the center of each. The first boat that completes the task and crosses the finish line wins. You can vary play by allowing paddlers take a shot at throwing the object into the circle from a distance, rather than having to paddle to it. Impose some type of penalty if they miss, such as having to perform a maneuver, sing a song, or count to 30.

#53: Push Ball Relay

Craft: Canoes, kayaks

Skill Level: Good boat control

Water: Flatwater

Playing Area: Large clear open area

Supplies: Boats, paddles, one large beach ball per boat (Rubber playground balls may also be used.)

Skills: Steering, turning, reacting to execute correct strokes and maneuvers, precision

Establish start and finish lines. You should have a good distance between the start and end. Have participants arrange boats so that bows are on the start line, facing the direction of the finish line, with about four to six feet between boats. Each boat has a ball.

The object of this relay is to use the boat to push the ball from the start to the finish line. At the start signal, the ball is dropped (not thrown) into the water at the tip of the bow. Paddlers push the ball using the boat. Only the boat may touch and push the ball. If the ball gets stuck under the boat, paddles may be used to dislodge. The first boat to get across the finish line wins. Vary the game by allowing paddles to also be used to push the ball.

#54: Steal the Bacon

Craft: Kayaks
Skill Level: Any
Water: Flatwater
Playing Area: Large clear open area
Supplies: Kayaks, buoys, large foam ball (or sponge)
Skills: Steering, turning, balance

Establish a playing area with defined boundaries, including an end line on opposite sides which will be the safe zone for each team. Set a buoy to indicate each safe zone, and also place a buoy in the center of the playing area. The total size of the playing area will depend on how many boats are playing, as well as the paddling skill of participants. Make the area smaller for novice boaters, and larger for experienced paddlers. Participants are hand-paddling for this game.

The object is for each team to steal the bacon and make it back to their safe zone without getting tagged. Divide the group into two equal teams. Have each team of kayaks line up on the center line, facing each other, with about 10 feet between the two lines of boats. Their "home base" or safe zone will be behind them. Starting with one team, have the paddlers number themselves off (from one, two, three, etc.) until everyone has a number. Then, starting at the opposite end, have the other team number themselves off in the same manner. When the two teams are facing each other, the two players who are both number one should be on opposite ends of the lines, not facing directly across from each other.

The instructor throws the bacon (ball or sponge) into the center of the lineup and calls a number. The paddler from each team who has the number called hand-paddles out to try to be the one who gets to the bacon first (other team members may not obstruct their passage). Whoever gets the bacon first becomes the boat being chased, and the other paddler becomes "it." The paddler with the bacon has to make it back to the safe zone without being tagged in order to score a point. If he makes it to the safe zone, his team gets the point. If he is tagged, the other team gets the point.

As soon as the numbered paddler touches the bacon, the other paddlers from both teams may engage in play. The team members for the team with the bacon are trying to block the "it" from tagging the bacon-carrying boat and create a path of safe passage to the safe zone. The members of the "it" team are trying to help the "it" tag the bacon-stealer.

Blocking can only be done with boats blocking boats. Boat-to-paddler contact and paddler-to-paddler contact is not permitted. Illegal moves, such as holding, intentionally capsizing members of the other team, and so forth, can be penalized with points taken away or given to the other team.

#55: What's the Time, Mr. Wolf?

Craft: Canoes, kayaks
Skill Level: Any
Water: Flatwater
Playing Area: Large clear open area
Supplies: Boats, paddles, buoys
Skills: Steering, turning, reacting and executing strokes and maneuvers

Establish two end lines with a good distance between them. Mark the end lines with buoys. Select one boat to be Mr. Wolf. The rest of the paddlers are piggies. Position Mr. Wolf at one end line, facing away from the playing area. The piggies line up with the bows on the line at the other end of the playing area, facing the direction of Mr. Wolf.

To start the game, in unison, the piggies ask loudly, "What time is it, Mr. Wolf?" and Mr. Wolf will reply by saying a time, such as, "It's 10 o'clock." The piggies then have to paddle forward toward Mr. Wolf the same number of strokes as the time (so, 10 strokes forward for 10 o'clock, six strokes forward for 6 o'clock, and so on). Once stopped, the piggies ask again, "What time is it, Mr. Wolf?" and Mr. Wolf will reply by saying another time, and the piggies paddle forward that same number of strokes.

They continue to repeat this question-and-answer cycle, until such time as Mr. Wolf feels that the piggies are close enough to eat (tag), at which point his reply to the question "What time is it, Mr. Wolf?" will be "It's dinner time!" At this point, the wolf turns around and paddles toward the piggies, trying to tag them, and the piggies scatter and try to paddle back to their end line, which is their home base. Piggies who make it back past the home base without being tagged are safe, and play again. Piggies who are tagged are now in Mr. Wolf's freezer and are frozen, bobbing around in place in the playing area until the game is over (creating obstacles to have to paddle around for both the other pigs and the wolf).

Mr. Wolf is not allowed to look behind him during the game, and so will give times based on where he estimates the piggies to be located. Mr. Wolf's objective is the get the piggies as close as possible, before chasing them. The game ends when all of the piggies are in the freezer. The last piggie left becomes the new wolf. To vary the game, the first piggie tagged in each round becomes the new wolf, and no piggies are frozen.

#56: Spud

Craft: Canoes, kayaks
Skill Level: Any
Water: Flatwater
Playing Area: Large clear open area
Supplies: Boats, paddles, beach ball (or large foam ball or sponge)
Skills: Reacting and executing strokes and maneuvers, quickly stopping

Establish a playing area with defined boundaries. Have boats count off until all boats have a number. All of the boats gather around in a cluster in the middle of the playing area. The instructor throws the ball high in the air and yells "Spud in the air, number X," calling out a number of a boat. At this point, all of the boats that do not have that number try to scatter as far away from the ball as possible. The boat with that number quickly paddles toward the ball and catches it. As soon as the paddler touches the ball with his hand, he yells "Freeze," at which point all of the other boats must stop. For fair play, it is important that the other players actually *stop* their craft, not just stop paddling and continue to drift.

The object is for the boat holding the ball to tag another person with it by throwing it at them. If he throws and hits the person, the person he hits gets a letter. If he throws and misses, he gets a letter. (No points are given for catching the ball). The letters are S-P-U-D. The first letter a boat gets is "S", then it would be "P," and so on, until they become a spud! The boat that is not a spud, or has the least number of letters when everyone else is a spud, is the winner

Depending on the group you are working with, and the size of the playing area, you may elect to allow the "it" boat to hand-paddle a set number of strokes toward another boat, so they can get closer in order to have success in tagging them.

#57: Pontoon Platoon

Craft: Canoes, kayaks
Skill Level: Any
Water: Flatwater
Playing Area: Large clear open area
Supplies: Boats, paddles, buoys or other markers
Skills: Executing strokes and maneuvers, improving communication for tandem boats

For this activity, boats "raft up" with other boats, and navigate paddling through an obstacle course. To start, each boat pairs up with another boat of the same kind, gunwale-to-gunwale, hull-to-hull. While navigating the course, the two boats must be touching side-to-side at all times. Paddlers have to hold on to each others' boats with either body parts or paddles. Boats cannot be tied (chained, clipped, taped, bungied, or similar) together. Time participants through the course, and then work on skills to improve their times. Vary the activity by having boats paddle the obstacle course in groups of three, then four, until the whole group is one big pontoon. Add more challenge and have teams paddle the course backward. Various strokes and maneuvers can be practiced with this activity.

The course set-up can be as simple or complex as desired. In addition to buoys, utilize bridges, pilings, or docks when possible. In addition to going around, under, and through obstacles, you can add challenge by having participants compete certain maneuvers, such has having to spin the boat a set number of times at a location, or change positions.

iStockphoto/Thinkstock

#58: Put Down My Coconuts

Craft: Canoes, kayaks

Skill Level: Any

Water: Flatwater

Playing Area: Large clear open area

Supplies: Boats, paddles, five balls or ducks (or coconuts), four buoys, four inner tubes (Ring buoys, hoops, or child's inflatable swim rings will also work in place of the inner tubes.)

Skills: Executing strokes and maneuvers

The object of this game is for a team to collect three coconuts. Establish a large, square-shaped playing area. Place a buoy at each of the four corners of the playing area. Then, attach an inner tube to each buoy, so that it is lying flat, floating on the water (but attached to the buoy so it won't drift away). (You can also set the inner tubes with line and weights as their own buoys, as long as they are lying on the water, not standing on end.) The inner tubes serve as floating "corrals" to keep the coconuts from drifting away. Put the five balls (coconuts) in the center of the playing area. Divide the group into four even teams, and assign each team to one of the inner tubes in each corner.

When the game starts, each team tries to get three coconuts into their inner tube:

- They can remove coconuts from the center of the playing area, or from the other team's inner tubes.
- A team can only move one coconut at a time.
- Teams cannot guard their inner tubes.
- Coconuts may never be thrown.

#59: Square Dance

Craft: Canoes, kayaks
Skill Level: Any
Water: Flatwater
Playing Area: Large clear open area
Supplies: Boats, paddles
Skills: Reacting to execute strokes and maneuvers

Divide the group into four equal teams. Arrange the group so that each team is lined up to create one side of a square, paddlers facing in to the center. Be sure to give everyone plenty of space. Once you have a square shape assembled, paddle your boat to the center of the square.

The object of this game is for the boats on all four sides of the square to remain in the same position in relationship to the person in the middle. The team that is at the bow of your boat at the start of the game must always stay at the bow end of your boat. The team that is at the stern of your boat must always stay at the stern end of your boat. The team that is on the port side of your boat must always stay on the port side. The team that is on the starboard side of your boat must always stay on the starboard side.

When you move into a new position, the boats in the square must collectively move as quickly as possible so they are in the same position as before. You can turn quickly or slowly, a little or a lot.

#60: Stalker

Craft: Canoes, kayaks
Skill Level: Any
Water: Flatwater
Playing Area: Large clear open area
Supplies: Boats, paddles
Skills: Executing strokes and maneuvers

Stalker is a game where only the paranoid (and sneaky) survive. Each paddler or boat is a stalker, who will randomly select another boat to observe. Prior to playing, determine if tandem boats will work together to stalk the same boat, or if each paddler will stalk his own victim separately.

Establish a large, open playing area. To start the game, have everyone silently paddle around the playing area, moving about in various directions. At the signal, they quietly begin stalking their victim. As they paddle around, they are to be sure to keep their boat in sight at all times, while being careful not the let that person know they are stalking him. Players should try not to be obvious, and should make it difficult by paddling in and out of the crowd, and so forth. Let everyone paddle around for a few minutes, and then have players try to figure out who is stalking them. At the same time players are trying to figure out who is stalking them, they have to remember to keep an eye on the boat they are stalking. At the end of the activity, have paddlers try to identify their stalkers. Some paddlers may have multiple stalkers, and some may have had none, but were paranoid anyway.

7

Games and Activities for Transitioning to Moving Water

Jupiterimages

The activities in this chapter are suitable for paddlers who have mastered fundamental strokes and maneuvers for propulsion, steering, and turning and are ready to transfer skills learned on flatwater to moving water and whitewater.

Leaning

Many of the activities in this chapter have a focus on developing leaning skills. Those participants new to paddling often equate leaning with tipping over. However, to truly master paddling, participants need to gain an understanding that balance and weight shifts are as important as paddling strokes. This factor becomes especially critical as they transition to moving water and whitewater.

The key is to lean the boat, not the body. The paddler's center of gravity should remain over the centerline. For a proper lean in a canoe, the paddler adjusts his weight by shifting it to one knee, tilting the boat up on one side while keeping his body over the boat. For a proper lean in a kayak, the paddler adjusts his weight by shifting the hips, tilting the boat up on one side while keeping his body over the boat. The wrong way in both craft is to keep the hull flat (which novice paddlers prefer as this technique has a more stable feel) and lean the body out over the water.

Prior to conducting activities that include leaning, participants should have instruction in boat leaning appropriate for the craft they are paddling, and have had an opportunity to try these skills. The activities can be used for practice.

Stationary/Static Strokes

In several activities, paddlers practice executing stationary strokes (sometimes also referred to as "static" strokes), such as the duffek (or "post" stroke), stationary draws, stationary prys, and such, in order to perform turns. Stationary (or static) strokes are when the paddler turns the boat by "planting" or "sticking" the paddle in the water near the bow and letting the momentum of the boat (or the current in whitewater) pull the boat around the paddle.

The specific stationary/static strokes to be taught and practiced are not defined in the activities; this aspect is left to the discretion of the instructor. The strokes and sequencing that you elect to instruct and use for these activities will vary based on the type of craft, as well as the skill level of the participants.

#61: Balance Buoy

Craft: Canoes, kayaks
Skill Level: Ready to practice leaning
Water: Flatwater
Playing Area: Large clear open area
Supplies: Boats, paddles
Skills: Leaning, proper body position
Note: Capsize during this activity is fairly common, and should be planned for.

In this activity, participants feel the difference between a proper lean, where a paddler keeps his body weight over the boat, and the wrong way to lean. Space boats at least 10 feet apart to avoid any collisions or contact injuries if a boat capsizes. Paddles are stowed during these activities.

First, have participants practice how not to lean by doing the "bell-buoy" lean. The bell-buoy lean is done by sitting up straight in the boat and keeping the body straight and stiff while rocking the boat from side to side, like a bell-buoy in the ocean. Participants in canoes may hold the gunwales as they rock side to side. As participants become committed to performing this lean, those participants in canoes will find that their body weight goes out over the gunwale, and expect that at least some will capsize. Novice kayakers typically flip over quite easily. After discussing what went wrong and why, have participants practice correct leaning, specific to the craft they are paddling.

Hemera/Thinkstock

#62: Charm School

Craft: Canoes, kayaks
Skill Level: Good boat control, ability to execute steering and turning
Water: Flatwater
Playing Area: Large clear open area
Supplies: Boats, paddles, buoys, rubber ducks (one per paddler)
Skills: Proper body position and center of gravity in leans and turns

Prior to conducting this activity, participants should have instruction in boat leaning skills appropriate for the craft they are paddling, and have had an opportunity to practice these skills.

In this activity, participants practice keeping their weight over the boat while turning and leaning. As a tool in developing these skills, paddlers practice turns and leans while balancing a rubber duck on their head. The concept equates to the charm school skill of balancing a book on your head while walking. Too much lean of the head, and the book (or in this case, the rubber duck) slides off. The goal is to help paddlers learn to keep their head and body upright, while using their lower body and leaning the boat into the turns, rather than leaning their upper body out over the boat.

For the first couple of tries, have participants practice paddling forward without any leaning, to get the feel of keeping their body over the boat and balancing the duck. This technique also helps remind paddlers to sit upright in their boats.

Next, have participants spread out and practice the following. Paddle forward, gaining good forward momentum, and then initiate a turn. Lean into the turn, taking their paddles out of the water. Maintain the lean, and "ride the glide" (momentum) as the boat turns, without losing the duck. As they progress, have participants navigate through a series of buoys (as in #63: Serpentine), executing leans in the turns while balancing the duck on their head. To make it more interesting, you can also set this up as an obstacle course.

#63: Serpentine

Craft: Canoes, kayaks
Skill Level: Good boat control, ability to execute steering and turning
Water: Flatwater
Playing Area: Large clear open area
Supplies: Boats, paddles, buoys
Skills: Connecting strokes and maneuvers, stroke precision, turning, leaning, improving communication for tandem boats

In this activity, boats go through a series of buoys in much the same manner as race cars go through a series of cones. The turning dynamics and speed of the boats is determined by the distance the cones are set apart, vertically and horizontally. How you elect to set up the buoys is determined by the specific skills that the paddlers are working on. Buoys that are set farther apart give paddlers more time to react. Buoys placed closer together result in paddlers needing to execute "tighter" turning maneuvers, and with faster response time. Have a start line and a finish line. Time participants through the course, and then work on skills to improve their times.

Note that when paddlers working on static strokes and turns combined with leaning, such as learning maneuvers for U-turns and progressing to eddy turns, they will need distance to build up forward momentum, as well as distance between maneuvers to allow for the "lean and turn" to take place. Set buoys far enough apart to allow for both.

iStockphoto/Thinkstock

#64: Snakes and Eights

Craft: Canoes, kayaks

Skill Level: Good boat control, ability to execute steering and turning

Water: Flatwater or moving water

Playing Area: Large clear open area

Supplies: Boats, paddles, buoys

Skills: Connecting strokes, precision, turning, leaning, preparing for eddy turns and peelouts

The objective of this activity is to execute S-turns (snakes) and figure eights with the least number of strokes. Set up two buoys per S (or eight) to mark where turns are to be conducted. Have participants execute S-turns ("make snakes") and/or figure eights, and count how many paddle strokes it takes them to perform the maneuver. They then work to reduce this number.

The turning dynamics will be determined by the distance the cones are set apart. Buoys which are set farther apart give paddlers more time to react and more room to paddle. Buoys placed closer together result in paddlers needing to execute "tighter" turning maneuvers. On flatwater, gaining forward momentum before executing the turns will be important, so be sure to allow for enough room ahead of the turning markers.

When S-turns and figure eights are conducted on flatwater, the focus will be on stroke precision and efficiency, and adding and increasing lean. As participants progress to moving water, maneuvers will also include speed and angle.

#65: Gator Turns

Craft: Canoes, kayaks
Skill Level: Executing stationary (static) strokes for turning
Water: Flatwater or moving water
Playing Area: Large clear open area
Supplies: Boats, paddles, buoys
Skills: Stationary strokes, turning, leaning, preparing for eddy turns and peelouts

In this activity, paddlers practice executing stationary/static strokes in order to perform U-turns. Before starting the activity, tell the participants this story (or make up something of your own): "You are paddling down the Walla Walla waterway on a beautiful, calm, sunny day, enjoying a fun outing. You have brought your favorite pet poodle Fifi along for the ride. Fifi loves being in the boat, and is happily wagging her tail, content with the sheer enjoyment felt by a poodle out on a paddle. Unbeknownst to you, however, is that up ahead, the waterway is infested with huge, killer alligators. And, of course *everyone* knows that an alligator's all-time favorite meal is poodle. Unable to turn back, you must now execute quick U-turns to escape certain peril, or poor little Fifi is a goner!"

To conduct this activity, participants paddle forward straight toward a buoy (the gator), gaining good, fast, forward momentum. Just as they reach the gator, as a strategic get-away from certain doom, they "plant" (or "stick") the appropriate stationary stroke, lean, and allow the momentum to carry the boat through the U-turn, just in time so no one in the boat is eaten. If their boat touches the gator, well, it's lights out for poor little Fifi. Ideally, set out enough buoys so that only one or two boats are practicing at any one spot, and can have continuous practice.

#66: Apple, Orange, Banana

Craft: Tandem canoes

Skill Level: Executing stationary (static) strokes for turning

Water: Flatwater (can also be used in slow moving water for beginning eddy turn practice)

Playing Area: Large clear open area

Supplies: Boats, paddles, buoys

Skills: Stationary strokes, turning, leaning, connecting strokes and maneuvers, partner communication, synchronizing strokes, preparing for eddy turns and peelouts

In this activity, paddlers practice executing stationary/static strokes combined with synchronized dynamic turning strokes in order to perform U-turns. Apple, Orange, Banana is not the activity, per se, but rather is a verbal timing tool that is used to help paddlers practice synchronizing their strokes.

To start, participants paddle forward straight toward a buoy, gaining good, fast, forward momentum. As they near the point where they are going to begin the turn, they count down the last three forward strokes ("Three, two, one"), and then begin using the strokes required to execute the turn, which starts on the cue "Apple." The change from calling out numbers to using "Apple, Orange, Banana" helps paddlers discern where the forward strokes used to gain momentum end and where the turning strokes begin. The intent of the verbal cues is to help the paddlers synchronize their turning strokes. Ideally, the last turning stroke required to complete the full U-turn will end together with "Orange," and then, together at "Banana," the paddlers transition back to forward strokes.

The specific turning strokes and combinations to be taught and practiced are not defined in this activity; this aspect is left to the discretion of the instructor. The strokes that you elect to instruct and use for these activities will vary based on the teaching objective as well as the skill level of the participants. The following scenarios are simply examples of possible combinations. The actual combinations that you select to put together should reflect the learning outcomes desired.

Example #1: Bow paddling on the left, stern paddling on the right. U-turn to the canoe's off-side (left).

Bow Paddler
- Apple: Stationary stroke planted at the bow.
- Orange: Continues to hold stationary stroke as the momentum of the boat pulls the boat around the paddle.
- Banana: Transitions to complete dynamic turning stroke, such as drawing in at the bow, and then will connect this move to a forward stroke.

Stern Paddler
- Apple: Forward quarter sweep
- Orange: Forward quarter sweep
- Banana: Forward

Example #2: Bow paddling on the left, stern paddling on the right. U-turn to the canoe's onside (right).

Bow Paddler
- Apple: Cross stationary stroke planted at the bow.
- Orange: Continues to hold cross stationary stroke as the momentum of the boat pulls the boat around the paddle.
- Banana: Transitions to complete dynamic turning stroke, such as drawing in at the bow, and then will connect this move to a forward stroke.

Stern Paddler
- Apple: Reverse quarter sweep
- Orange: Reverse quarter sweep
- Banana: Forward

#67: Barrel Racing

Craft: Canoes, kayaks
Skill Level: Good boat control, ability to execute steering and turning
Water: Flatwater
Playing Area: Large clear open area
Supplies: Boats, paddles, buoys
Skills: Connecting strokes and maneuvers, stroke precision, turning, leaning, improving communication and synchronized paddling for tandem boats

In this activity, paddlers maneuver to complete a cloverleaf pattern around three barrels (buoys) in the fastest time. Paddlers must pay attention to detail while maneuvering at speed, and precision paddling is required to win.

Paddlers start from a distance behind the start line and begin paddling as fast as possible so that they are at top speed when they cross the start line. Timing begins when the boat crosses the start line, and ends when the pattern has been successfully executed and the boat crosses the finish line. To have the most success in this activity, paddlers must rate their speed at the right moment to enter the correct path to make a perfect turn, and turns should be a relatively even half circle around the barrel.

Bouys are set out in a triangle shape, with approximatley the same distance between each buoy. The cloverleaf pattern is shown in Figure 67-1.

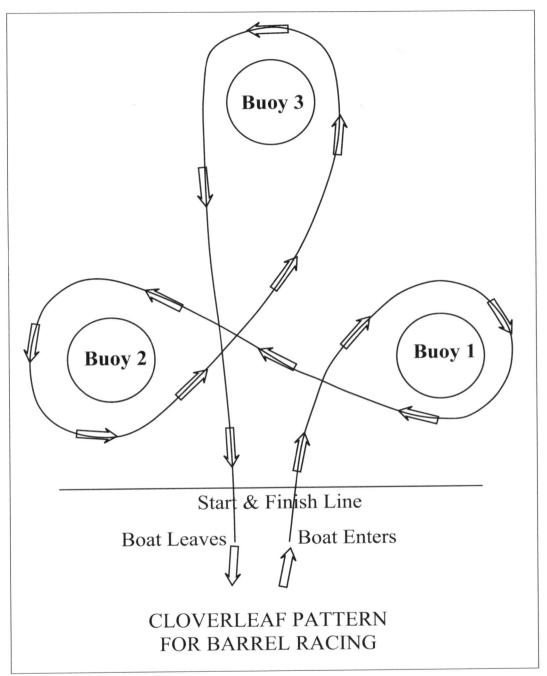

Buoy 3

Buoy 2

Buoy 1

Start & Finish Line

Boat Leaves | Boat Enters

CLOVERLEAF PATTERN
FOR BARREL RACING

Figure 67-1

#68: Go With the Flow

Craft: Canoes, kayaks
Skill Level: Any
Water: Flatwater
Playing Area: Large clear open area
Supplies: Boats, paddles, buoys, or other markers
Skills: Connecting and improving strokes and maneuvers, leaning, balance, timing, using momentum

The object of this activity is to go through an untimed obstacle course, using lean, balance, timing, and momentum to carry the boat through all of the turns; "ride the glide" to go with the flow.

In the course's straightaways, participants paddle forward, gaining good, fast, forward momentum. Then, as they reach a turn, they take their paddle(s) out of the water, lean the boat, and allow the momentum to carry the boat through the turn. The course set-up can be as simple or complex as desired, but should alternate between straightaways and turns.

#69: Ferry-ly We Roll Along

Craft: Canoes, kayaks
Skill Level: Ready to practice ferrying
Water: Light, slow-moving water with some current
Playing Area: Large clear open area, with some slow current
Supplies: Boats, paddles, throwables (optional: surveyor's tape or caution tape)
Skills: Ferrying

The object of this activity is for paddlers to ferry from one side of the waterway to the other, collecting one object which has been placed on each side each time they cross.

Place an equal number of objects on each side of the waterway, in a straight line across from each other. Objects should be where the paddler can easily reach out and collect them. If the bank is not accessible, is covered with poison ivy, or the like, and you can't put out any objects, try looping short ribbons of surveyors tape on a low hanging branch for them to collect. The boat that collects its objects in the shortest amount of time wins.

For this activity to work, the speed of the water has to be flowing fast enough so participants cannot simply paddle straight forward from one side to the other, like they would on flatwater.

#70: It's an Eddy, Eddie

Craft: None required; dry land activity

Skill Level: Learning about eddy turns and peelouts

Water: Land game

Playing Area: Indoors or outdoors (A paved, concrete, or tiled floor is ideal.)

Supplies: Paddles (one per person), masking tape or sidewalk chalk, items which can be used to set up the on-land eddies, such as cones, chairs, trash cans, boxes, and balls

Skills: Fundamental steps in executing eddy turns and peelouts, better understanding of reading the "eddy line" and river current

One of the challenges for those participants who are brand new to whitewater is being able to read the water, understand current differentials, and *find the eddy line*. It's often easy for seasoned paddlers and instructors to forget that the anatomy of an eddy can be a complex topic which is hard to understand (after all, doesn't everything in the river flow downstream?). This activity helps to introduce the fundamental concepts of eddy turns and peelouts, in a *very* back-to-basics manner (and without any on-water distractions, or the underlying stress or fear of failure often encountered when novice participants move to whitewater).

Set up a series of fake eddies, using a combination of solid items (cones, boxes, trashcans) as the obstacles (rocks) that will create the eddy. Define the direction of water flow with tape or chalk arrows, but don't add the current lines yet.

Activity Part #1: With the group, start with the first obstacle, and discuss how the water might be flowing around it. Using the sidewalk chalk or tape (depending on the floor surface), have participants identify and draw/tape three things: the current that is flowing downstream around the object; the current that is flowing back upstream, filling in the depression below the object; and the location where these two currents meet, i.e., the line where the current is flowing in opposite directions—the eddy line. (If you have multiple colors of chalk or tape, it's an added visual bonus to do each in a different color.) Have participants do this same task for each of the on-land eddies you have created.

Activity Part #2: Have participants air-paddle to perform eddy turns and peelouts. This dry land set-up is a great way to introduce the concepts of eddy turns and peelouts. If they have already been practicing on water, have them walk through their strokes and maneuvers, including adding angle and lean. This activity is also a good way to introduce the concepts of current differential and why leaning is important.

8

Games and Activities for Moving Water

Photo Courtesy of The U.S. Coast Guard

Safety Reminder: Select locations where each participant is paddling within their limits. *Only* paddle and play games where water conditions are suitable to the skill level of the participants, including being able to "read" the water and effectively steer and propel their boat under control.

#71: Downriver Racing

Craft: Kayaks, canoes

Skill Level: Ability to paddle on moving water

Water: Moving water, or easy whitewater

Playing Area: Short stretch with some variation, such as rapids, small standing waves, and such appropriate to the skill level of the participants

Supplies: Boats, paddles

Skills: Executing strokes and maneuvers

Select a section of water and establish start and finish lines. One boat paddles the course at a time. Time participants through the course, and then work on skills to improve their times. Add challenge by having paddlers execute maneuvers such as eddy turns, peelouts, or ferrying.

#72: Upriver Racing

Craft: Kayaks, canoes

Skill Level: Ability to paddle on moving water

Water: Moving water, or easy whitewater

Playing Area: Short stretch with some variation, such as rapids, small standing waves, and such appropriate to the skill level of the participants

Supplies: Boats, paddles

Skills: Executing strokes and maneuvers, understanding the effect of currents

Racing downstream is one thing; racing upstream is a completely different challenge. For this activity to work, the speed of the water has to be flowing fast enough so participants cannot simply paddle forward like they would on flatwater. Select a section of water, and establish start and finish lines. One boat paddles the course at a time. Time participants through the course, and then work on skills to improve their times.

#73: Elevator Up

Craft: Kayaks, canoes
Skill Level: Ability to paddle on moving water
Water: Easy whitewater
Playing area: Long stretch of water with plenty of variation—such as rock gardens, eddies, several rapids, chutes, small standing waves, and such—where conditions are suitable to the skill level of the participants
Supplies: Boats, paddles
Skills: Executing strokes and maneuvers

The bottom (downstream) end of the stretch is the "ground floor." The top (upstream) end of the stretch is the "top floor." Boats are the "elevators." Participants start on the ground floor and see how high up they can get their elevator. The goal is getting to the top floor. If they get "washed out," then they have to come back to the ground floor to start over. To add even more challenge, time participants through the course, and then work on skills to improve their times.

#74: Rock'n'Roll

Craft: Kayaks, canoes
Skill Level: Ability to paddle on moving water
Water: Moving water, or easy whitewater
Playing Area: Short stretch with some variation, such as easy rapids, small standing waves, and such
Supplies: Boats
Skills: Leaning, balance, timing, working with the momentum of the boat, becoming more intuitive and developing a feel for the boat

In this activity, participants navigate a stretch of water using balance, timing, and leaning, rather than using a paddle. Select a stretch of easy-moving water, and designate a start point and end point. At the start line, participants stow their paddles and proceed to navigate their way downstream by using their body "in sync" with the boat, relying on timing, balance, leaning, and using the boat's momentum. The stretch of water needs to be slow and easy enough so participants have success with the activity (and not just get washed downstream), but diverse enough to add some challenge, such as having some small standing waves, current change, and so forth. Make sure the stretch is not just a chute where all boats will simply ride through easily. As participants improve, select more difficult areas to run.

#75: Eyes Wide Shut

Craft: Solo canoes, solo kayaks
Skill Level: Ability to paddle on moving water
Water: Moving water, easy whitewater
Playing Area: Slow, flat stretch or moving water without any hazards
Supplies: Boats, paddles
Skills: Becoming more intuitive in paddling skills, developing a feel for the boat

The objective of this activity is to help participants feel when to use corrective strokes. Select start and end points. Participants begin to navigate the slow downstream course, then close their eyes for a count of five, then open them and see if they have stayed on course. They adjust, paddle a few strokes, and close their eyes again. Participants keep repeating the exercise, and try to increase the amount of time they can paddle with their eyes closed.

Photodisc

#76: Sheep and Wolves

Craft: Kayaks, canoes
Skill Level: Ability to paddle on moving water
Water: Easy whitewater stretch, with rocks and eddies
Playing Area: Stretch with some variation, plenty of easy eddies, appropriate to the skill
level of the participants
Supplies: Boats, paddles
Skills: Executing strokes and maneuvers, eddy turns, peelouts, ferrying

This activity is a tag game that has participants paddling both up and down through a stretch of easy whitewater. The ideal playing location will be in a rock garden, or stretch of water where there are multiple eddies and small rapids, and lots of places for the wee sheep to hide. Be sure to select an area where paddlers can negotiate the water at their skill level.

Select one boat to be the wolf; the other boats are sheep. The wolf is chasing the sheep, trying to tag them, and the sheep are trying not to get tagged. Sheep are safe from the wolf when they are sitting in an eddy, but sheep grazing in the same eddy all day is boring for the wolf (and the sheep). So anytime the wolf says the following, "Little sheep, come out and play, you need to come—either "up" or "down"—the field today," all eddy-sitting sheep have to relocate. If the wolf says the sheep need to come down the field, they have to exit the eddy they are currently sitting in, paddle heading downstream, and find a new eddy to hide in, or keep paddling away from the wolf. If the wolf says the sheep need to come up the field, they have to exit the eddy and paddle upstream.

- Sheep don't have to simply sit in an eddy waiting. They can come and go at will. However, they have to exit an eddy is the wolf calls them out.
- Sheep may paddle anywhere in the designated playing area, and the wolf may chase them everywhere, except that a wolf may never enter an eddy that is occupied by sheep.
- More than one sheep may be in the same eddy.
- When a wolf catches a sheep, the sheep becomes another wolf.

#77: … And Then

Craft: Kayaks, canoes
Skill Level: Ability to paddle on moving water
Water: Easy whitewater
Playing Area: Long stretch of water with plenty of variation—such as rock gardens, eddies, several rapids, chutes, small standing waves, and such—where conditions are suitable to the skill level of the participants
Supplies: Boats, paddles
Skills: Executing strokes and maneuvers

This activity can be conducted downstream or upstream. Boats line up following the other. The boat at the front of the line performs a stroke or maneuver, which the boats following behind also perform, like in follow the leader. However, after doing so, the lead boat falls back to the end of the line, and the next boat in the progression becomes the new leader, and adds whatever strokes or maneuver it wishes, including being able to change the direction upstream or downstream, or changing the path of travel through the rapid set by the boat in front. After that boat has its turn, it falls to the back of the line … *And then* …

#78: Bow Balloon

Craft: Tandem kayaks, tandem canoes
Skill Level: Ability to paddle on moving water
Water: Easy whitewater
Playing Area: Long stretch of water with plenty of variation—such as rock gardens, eddies, several rapids, chutes, small standing waves, and such—where conditions are suitable to the skill level of the participants
Supplies: Boats, paddles, balloons
Skills: Executing strokes and maneuvers, communication, timing, balance, leaning

Set a clear course downstream through the rapid or rock garden. Add variety by including executing maneuvers, eddy turns, and such as possible. Demonstrate the course so that all participants know where to go. Hand each bow paddler three balloons. Have them blow up and tie off one balloon, keeping the other two as reserves. The bow paddler does not paddle during this activity. Rather, their job is to bounce the balloon continuously throughout the duration of the run. They are never allowed to hold their balloon as they go through the course. If they lose their balloon, or if the balloon lands in the water or on an object, establish a penalty. To have success with this activity, the pair must work together. To add more challenge, time participants through the course, and then work on skills to improve their times.

#79: The Gauntlet

Craft: Tandem kayaks, tandem canoes

Skill Level: Ability to paddle on moving water

Water: Easy whitewater

Playing Area: Long stretch of water with plenty of variation—such as rock gardens, eddies, several rapids, chutes, small standing waves, and such—where conditions are suitable to the skill level of the participants (For this game to be successful, the area needs to have lots of eddies.)

Supplies: Boats, paddles, foam balls, sponges, or other throwables (three per person)

Skills: Executing strokes and maneuvers

Divide the group into two equal teams. So teams can be identified, give at least one of the teams a blindfold or bandana to tie around their head or shoulder of their lifejacket. Pick which team will be "it" first. Issue three throwables to each person on the "it" team. Establish clear start and finish lines at the top and bottom of the stretch of water to be used.

The object of this game is for the "it" team to tag as many players from the opposing team as possible while they are making a downstream run. Paddlers are tagged by being hit with a ball thrown by the opposing team's players, and the same person can be tagged in succession by the same player. Passing balls to another team member is permitted. One point is issued per tag. However, the "it" teams players can only throw a ball if they are positioned in an eddy.

This game can be played several ways. The first variation is to start both teams at the top of the run at the same time. In this version, the players are racing each other downstream, with the "it" team trying to quickly navigate into the eddies so they can thrown their balls, while the team being chased is trying to get through the run without being tagged. In the second variation, the "it" team starts downstream, and the team being chased starts at the upstream end, with both teams starting at the same time. The "it" team has to paddle upstream to get into the eddies, while the downstream paddlers try to avoid running past them. In either version, teams change roles after an agreed upon number of runs. Note that it usually doesn't take long before players start working together to develop blocking, passing, and assisting strategies.

#80: Strainer Swim

Craft: None required; self-rescue swimming activity
Skill Level: Ability to paddle on moving water, good swimming skills
Water: Moving water to light easy whitewater
Playing Area: Current no stronger than Class I, water depth no deeper than waist deep
Supplies: Strong rope, 6- to 10-foot length of six-inch PVC pipe
Skills: Self-rescue in learning how to swim over a strainer

In this activity, paddlers will learn what to do in the event they encounter a strainer while swimming in current, such as after capsize. Prior to this activity, participants should have instruction in on-water hazards and be aware of what a strainer is and the dangers posed by them.

Explain to participants how to swim over a strainer:

- Swim toward the strainer head first with arms extended, ready to grab hold of the object (what is creating the strainer, such as the tree branch).
- Kick with your feet behind you at the surface.
- When you reach the strainer, kick *aggressively*, keeping your feet at the surface, and climb up onto, or over, the strainer.

For this activity, instructors use a long length of six-inch PVC pipe to simulate the strainer, which participants will practice swimming over, in the same manner as if it is a real strainer. Two people hold each end of the pipe at the surface, and one at a time participants practice swimming over it.

Safety Reminders:

- The area of water where this activity is conducted should be no more than waist deep, have no foot entrapment hazards, and be safe for those who are standing and holding the pipe.
- The PVC pipe must be at least six feet long.
- No hazards should be found immediately downstream from where the activity is conducted.
- Everyone should be wearing a properly fitting U.S. Coast Guard–approved lifejacket at all times during this activity, including those holding the pipe in place.

A line can be threaded through the pipe and tied off at shore to assist in holding the pipe (make sure the line has enough tension to keep the pipe at the surface while participants are swimming over it).

9

Games and Activities for Using Boating as Teambuilding

Maria Teijeiro

Canoes and kayaks can be a great tool to use for facilitating teambuilding activities with groups. Boats are often an underutilized resource in programs, often because operators don't realize the canoes and kayaks they already own can be utilized for the same types of learning outcomes typically offered using initiatives equipment or ropes courses.

In order to be most effective, these activities require the same type of skilled facilitation that would be utilized for teambuilding games and problem-solving initiatives on land. The approach and philosophy associated with these types of teambuilding activities is different than traditional teaching scenarios. People using these activities for the purpose of teambuilding are encouraged to seek training in facilitation, specifically including processing and debriefing, from an experiential adventure education training organization.

#81: Objects Up

Craft: Kayaks or tandem canoes*
Skill Level: Any
Water: Flatwater
Playing Area: Clear open area
Supplies: Boats, beach balls, or large balloons

Participants will be hand-paddling for this game. (Due to the risk of contact injury, paddles should never be used to hit the ball.) The object of this game is to work together to keep as many beach balls or balloons up in the air as possible at the same time. Gather boats into a cluster and throw up the first balloon or beach ball. After a few moments, add another, then another. Vary the game by using only one beach ball or balloon, counting how many total times the group can put it back up in the air. Work to set a world record. You can also set limits that the same paddler may not hit the same ball more than once in a row; the ball must be hit by someone else before a paddler can hit the same ball again.

---

*The activity may be modified to be used with tandem canoes. The bow paddler stows his paddle and uses his hands to hit the ball, while the stern paddler maneuvers the boat to keep the bow paddler in position.

#82: Fish Sticks

Craft: Canoes, kayaks

Skill Level: Good boat control

Water: Flatwater

Playing Area: Large clear open area

Supplies: Boats, paddles, buoys, four inner tubes (ring buoys, hoops, child's inflatable swim rings, or plastic laundry basket will also work in place of the inner tubes), large assortment of throwables

Note: Capsizing and boat collisions are common. If a boat capsizes during play, stop play, execute rescue, and then resume play from where everyone was.

This teambuilding activity requires a minimum of 8 to 10 boats to play (more is better). Establish a large rectangular-shaped playing area with clearly defined boundaries (see Figure 82-1). Place a buoy at each of the four corners of the playing area. Then, attach an inner tube to each buoy so that it is lying flat, floating on the water (but attached to the buoy so it won't drift away). (An alternative is to set the inner tubes with line and weights as their own buoys, as long as they are lying on the water, not standing on end.) The inner tubes serve as floating "corrals" to keep the throwables from drifting away. Next, put an assortment of throwables in the center of two of the inner tubes. Throwables are placed in one tube at one end, and in another at the other end, on the same side of the playing area. These tubes are the "home" hoops. The same number of throwable items should be in each. The two remaining empty inner tubes are the "scoring" hoops.

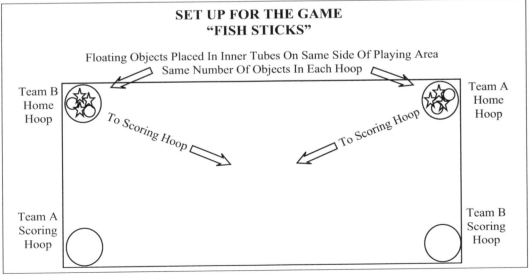

Figure 82-1

Divide the group into two teams. The object of the game is for each team to transport the items from their team's "home hoop" to their "scoring hoop," which is diagonally across on the opposite end of the playing area. The team with the most objects in their scoring hoop at the end of play wins. Of course, this game isn't as straightforward as it sounds:

- Only one object may be transported by a boat at a time.
- The other team may steal objects from the opposing teams "home" hoop and move it to their own "home" hoop. Only one object may be stolen and transported at a time.
- Stolen objects must first be transported to and be deposited in the stealing teams "home" hoop. From there, the object can then be transported to the scoring hoop cannot. Stolen objects cannot go directly to the opposing teams "scoring" hoop.
- Paddles may not be used to deflect people or as "bats" to deflect objects.

To find success, teams must work together to develop strategies to guard their home hoops from thieves, acquire objects from the other teams home hoops, and transport objects to the scoring hoop. The key to winning is cooperation, which is not usually obvious at the start. In the first rounds of play, facilitators can expect some fast action play and competitive behaviors, including hearing "Oh fish sticks!" when an opposing team member steals an object. This activity requires active facilitation to guide the players to work together as a team, and to encourage cooperative behavior between teams.

iStockphoto/Thinkstock

#83: Martian Meteor

Craft: Tandem canoes, tandem kayaks

Skill Level: Good boat control

Water: Flatwater

Playing Area: Large clear open area

Supplies: Boats, paddles, two inner tubes (ring buoys or child's inflatable swim rings will also work), one beach ball (rubber playground ball may be preferable in windy conditions), two buoys

Place each buoy a distance away from the other. Then, attach an inner tube to each buoy, so that it is floating on the water, but won't drift away. (An alternative is to set the inner tubes with line and weights as their own buoys, as long as they are lying on the water, not standing on end.) Place the beach ball so that it is sitting in the hole of one of the inner tubes.

Instruct participants that a meteor from Mars (ball) has fallen to Earth and is contaminated with radiation. The only hope for the survival of Earth is for the group to move the meteor from the temporary holding facility (inner tube #1) to the safety of the radiation containment unit (inner tube #2). The only way to move the meteor safely is to use their "meteor movers" (paddles), which have a special radiation-protective barrier. If the meteor touches any other object—such as boats or hands—the radiation will melt it, and it becomes unusable. If the meteor comes in contact with the water, the water becomes contaminated, and the group has to start over.

Photo Courtesy of The U.S. Coast Guard

#84: Flash Frozen Fish

Craft: Canoes, kayaks
Skill Level: Good boat control
Water: Flatwater
Playing Area: Large clear open area
Supplies: Boats, paddles, one inner tube (a ring buoy or child's inflatable swim ring will also work), a large assortment (50 or more) of plastic balls or throwables (The objects don't have to be the same—you just need a lot of them.)

The object of this teambuilding activity is for participants to collect all of the fish and return them to their fish pond as quickly as possible. Determine an approximate playing area, keeping in mind that this will shift as the balls drift as they float around on the surface. Set a buoy somewhere at the edge of the playing areas, and attach an inner tube to it so that it is floating on the water, but won't drift away. (An alternative is to set the inner tube with line and weight as its own buoy, as long as it is lying flat on the water, not standing on end.) A more challenging variation is to simply throw the inner tube out just before the start of game play and allow it to also drift about. Distribute the balls so that they are floating all around the playing area. If it's windy or wave or current action is present, throw these out on to the water at the start of play; otherwise, the objects may travel too far from the playing area. Keep some distance between the inner tube and where the balls are scattered on the water. To start play, assemble the boats in a cluster, explain the rules, and let them begin.

The task is to move the fish (balls), which are swimming all over the playing area, to their fish pond (inner tube):

- As soon as a boat, person, or paddle touches a fish, or is touched by a fish, the boat they are paddling in becomes flash frozen in place.
- Only the boat itself is frozen and must remain in place, the people in the boat continue to play.
- Paddlers must remain in their own boat.
- The only objects permitted to come in physical contact with the fish are hands or paddles. Participants may not use other items they may have, such as flip flops, hats, water bottles, or such.

This activity typically takes several do-overs before the group starts working together as a team. Be sure to provide opportunities for the group to do some strategic planning on successive tries.

#85: Star Light, Star Bright

Craft: Canoes, kayaks
Skill Level: Any
Water: Flatwater
Playing Area: Large clear open area
Supplies: Boats, paddles, very long piece of yarn, line, or twine (Length must be suitable for number of boats participating.)

The object of this teambuilding activity is for the group to create the shape of a five-point star using the yarn/twine. The star must be well-formed and obvious. A paddler from every boat must be in contact with the line. After the group finds success, try the same activity with half of the participants blindfolded, or don't allow anyone to talk.

#86: The Paddler Party

Craft: Canoes, kayaks
Skill Level: Any
Water: Flatwater
Playing Area: Large clear open area
Supplies: Boats, paddles

Explain to the group that they—the Paddler Party—are great American pioneers who have set out in 1846 for California in a wagon train. They have to get their wagons across the rugged terrain of the Sierra Nevada as quickly as possible. If they become delayed, they risk becoming snowbound in the mountains, and may suffer the same fate as the Donner Party and have to resort to cannnibalism to survive.

Select a large open area, and establish start and finish lines. The object is to move the entire group of boats from the start to the finish as fast as possible.

- Only one person in the group may be paddling at any one time.
- All of the boats must be connected (touching another boat) at all times.
- If boats become disconnected, the group must go back to the start line.

Add variation by doing this activity with half of the participants blindfolded, or not allowing anyone to talk.

#87: Boat Shapes

Craft: Canoes, kayaks
Skill Level: Any
Water: Flatwater
Playing Area: Large clear open area
Supplies: Boats, paddles

The object of this teambuilding activity is for the group to work together to create various shapes on the water with their boats. Every boat must participate in making every shape.

Facilitator gives the group forms that they must organize into, such as "square" or "triangle," or the shape of a letter, such as "W." As participants progress, make the shapes more difficult, such as "right triangle," "trapezoid," or "octagon." Continue with more complex and creative shapes, such as the shape of a state, or objects, like a banana, car, or airplane. Alternatively, you can also create cards or posters with various abstract shapes drawn on them, which the paddlers have to replicate using their boats. Add variation by doing this activity with half of the participants blindfolded, or not allowing anyone to talk.

#88: Backwards Ball

Craft: Canoes, kayaks
Skill Level: Any
Water: Flatwater
Playing area: Large clear open area
Supplies: Boats, beach ball

The object of this teambuilding activity is to pass a ball backward from boat to boat in the least amount of time. Boats form a train line, so that the bow of one boat is touching the stern of the boat in front of it. The first paddler in the boat at the front of the line has the beach ball. At the start signal, he has to pass or throw it backward over his head to the next paddler behind him. That paddler must catch it, and then passes or throws it backward over his head to the next paddler behind him. This process is repeated until the ball reaches the last paddler at the end of the line. If the ball is dropped at any point, the group must restart. Time each attempt, and encourage the group to work together to increase their time. Work to set a world record. Be sure to provide opportunities for the group to do some strategic planning on successive tries. Add variation by doing this activity with some of the participants blindfolded, or don't allow anyone to talk.

#89: Zigball

Craft: Canoes, kayaks
Skill Level: Any
Water: Flatwater
Playing Area: Large clear open area
Supplies: Boats, two large foam balls or beach balls

The object of this teambuilding game is for the group to pass a ball between team members for an agreed number of rounds in the shortest time possible. This activity requires a minimum of eight boats to play, more is better. Divide the whole group of boats into two equal teams of boats. For the purpose of organizing, give each team a name such as "Red Team" and "Blue Team." Give at least one of the teams a blindfold or bandana to tie around their head or shoulder of their lifejacket. Then, have each team divide itself into two equal groups of boats by counting off by "ones" and "twos." These boats are still members of their original red or blue teams; this count-off is for the purpose of getting the game set up correctly. Have all of the "ones" from both teams cluster together and all of the "twos" from both teams cluster together. They then form a line, alternating members of each team (red, blue, red, blue, etc.). Each line of boats then faces each other, leaving about three to four feet open between lines. Each boat should be directly across from a boat of the opposing team, and has a boat from the opposing team on either side. No boats from the same team should be directly facing each other. Adjust the lines as needed. Give a ball to each team at the same end of the two lines.

At the game start, the end person with the ball from both teams passes it across diagonally to their team member who is diagonally opposite, and then they pass it on to their next teammate who is diagonally opposite, so that the ball is passed "zigzag" down the line. When it reaches the end, it is passed back up the line, and then back down, and so forth. Passing the ball from one end to the other continues for as many times as the group has agreed upon at the start of the game. Whichever team completes the rounds first wins. You can also set a whole group goal rather than having two teams compete against each other, they problem solve how to compete *with* each other.

As balls are zigzagging across, they will inevitably collide, causing both teams loss of time and frustration. Facilitators can use this activity as a good example of teams competing in the same marketplace trying to achieve the same objective at the same time, and the benefits of different competitive or cooperative models. Communication typically also becomes a challenge as team members begin shouting diagonally, and everyone is trying to talk over the others.

#90: Spin It to Win It

Craft: Canoes, kayaks
Skill Level: Any
Water: Flatwater
Playing Area: Large clear open area
Supplies: Boats, paddles, plus one extra empty boat

The object of this teambuilding activity is for the group to cooperate and work together to keep an empty boat spinning "in perpetual motion" for a set time limit. To start the game, set the empty boat out on the water, assemble the participants in a group, explain the rules, and let them begin. It is up to the group to determine how they want to assemble themselves. Before starting the first round of play, have the group determine an amount of time they will keep the boat spinning:

- The spinner boat must remain in spinning motion for the duration of time. If it is allowed to stop, the round is over and the group re-starts.
- The same solo paddler/paddlers from the same tandem boat may not spin the boat more than once in a row The spinner boat must be spun by at least two other paddlers/paddlers from two other boats before they can touch it again.
- Every solo paddler/every tandem boat must participate and take turns spinning the boat.

Encourage the group to work together to increase their time. Work to set a world record. Be sure to provide opportunities for the group to do some strategic planning on successive tries. Add variation by doing this activity with some of the participants blindfolded, or not allowing anyone to talk.

Hemera/Thinkstock

#91: Build-a-Boat Regatta

Craft: None
Skill Level: Any
Water: Flatwater
Playing Area: Large clear open area
Supplies: See the Supply Ideas sections that follow.
Note: Plan on lots of capsizing, boats falling apart, and sinking.

The object of this teambuilding activity is for each team to create a boat that will stay afloat, and successfully paddle it to and from a set location. Participants may only use the materials provided to build their boat, and each group should be issued the same supplies. Everyone on the team must participate in the design and building process. Instructor should determine how many paddlers the boat must accommodate (suggest each boat be designed to carry either one or two paddlers, but you can set this requirement as desired). To conduct the regatta, each boat departs from shore (or the side of the pool), paddles a distance around a buoy, and returns to the start point. You can also have a competition to see which boat is faster, holds the most weight, or floats the longest.

Those participants conducting this activity can determine how easy or complicated is it based on the parameters set for design and building materials provided. The more complex the building materials, the longer the activity takes. For example, the use of glue or paint requires time for the boats to dry, whereas the use of foam pool noodles and duck tape are fairly quick and easy to work with. The supplies listed are only suggestions; use your creativity, as well as what is available.

Supply Ideas for Basic Build-a-Boat

- Foam pool noodles
- Cardboard mailing tubes
- Styrofoam
- Sheets of bubble wrap
- PVC pipe
- Large plastic trash bags
- Duct tape
- Rope or twine
- Foam core board
- Balloons
- Bed sheets or fabric
- Cardboard sheets or boxes

Supply Ideas for Tom Sawyer–style Raft Build-a-Boat

- Logs and large long tree limbs (be sure participants don't cut down live trees) or pre-cut lumber
- Rope or twine

Supply Ideas for Cardboard Build-a-Boat

- Corrugated cardboard (boxes and/or large sheets)
- Long straight edge (rule, yardstick, measuring tape)
- Marking pens and pencils
- Duct tape
- Cutting implement (utility knife, box cutter)
- Binder clips or clamps

Note: Box cutters are a safer alternative to an open blade knife, especially if you are working with kids.

Add the following items for more advanced cardboard boat building:
- Wood glue
- Paint and brush/roller (outdoor paint)
- Quick-dry caulking (latex)
- Optional polyurethane for top coat

Note: This phase requires ample time to allow glue/paint/sealant to dry.

Games and Activities for Rainy Days and Dry Land Classroom

Paul Greggs/Liquid Lessons

As paddling is an outdoor pursuit, you will no doubt have times when the weather, water temperature, or other factors encountered in the natural environment impacts your ability to get the group on the water.

Rainy-day activities are a must-have in any instructor's bag of tricks. Having a back-up plan is really important in settings like summer camps, where staff are responsible to provide activities during the scheduled period regardless of the weather, or when on a trip with a group as you don't have the option to reschedule the boating activity for the day. And, of course, the longer the lightning lasts, the more you may have to cover in a dry-land setting.

Beyond environmental factors, other reasons to be ready to use dry-land activities may include:
- When participants are fatigued
- To meet the needs of participants with various learning style or varying abilities/ disabilities
- Limited time for participants to learn material which cannot be accomplished during the allotted (or safe) on-water paddling times
- Modification of an activity for safety reasons

The people supervising boating activities should create a set of lesson plans for bad weather days and indoor teaching times that are relevant and meaningful to the activity. (It's also handy to be prepared for mishaps, like when you and the paddlers show up at the lake, but the guy driving the boat trailer doesn't.)

#92: The Paddle Parts Song

Playing Area: Land, indoors or outdoors
Supplies: Canoe paddle (one per person)
Skills: Canoe paddle nomenclature, light stretching and warm-up

This song was created by the counselors at Camp Tweedale in Oxford, Pennsylvania, to teach the parts of the canoe paddle and provide some fun warm-up exercise in the process. The song is sung to the tune of "Head, Shoulders, Knees, and Toes."

Participants should be standing, with the canoe paddle in front of them, holding it in their right hand, with the tip resting on their right foot. As each paddle part is named in the song, they touch that part with the free hand. The paddle stays still, so participants will have to bend down to touch the blade and tip, adding some physical warm-up to the activity. After going through the song once, have participants switch to holding the paddle with their left hand, tip resting on their left foot, touching the parts as they are named with the right hand, and repeat the song. As they learn the words, increase the speed of the song, and keep switching sides between each verse. Continue to increase the speed until they can't manage to keep up with the song any longer. The words are as follows:

Grip, shaft, throat, and blade, throat and blade
Grip, shaft, throat, and blade, throat and blade
And tip, and powerface, and non-powerface
Grip, shaft, throat, and blade, throat and blade

#93: Air Paddling

Playing Area: A large open space, such as a gym, is ideal.

Supplies: Paddle (one per person), items which can be used to set up the paddling course, such as cones, chairs, trash cans, boxes, and balls

Skills: Reinforcement of concepts, review of strokes and maneuvers, improving partner communication

In this activity, participants will walk their way through a mock paddling course while air-paddling. The set-up can be as simple or complex as you want, or have time for. Include areas where participants have to execute specific maneuvers, such as turns, spins, and paddling backward. If your participants were learning eddy turns, be sure to include some fake eddies on your mock river. You can even throw in some mock hazards, which paddlers will have to react to. Participants can be included in the design and set-up, too.

As paddlers air-paddle their way down the fake river, they should be thinking about the various elements that would impact the boat if they were really paddling on water, such as paddle placement, starting and stopping the stroke in the correct place, leaning into turns, and such. Tandem partners should be communicating, telling each other which stroke they are using and why, and working to synchronize strokes. While the premise may be silly, some real opportunity for serious learning is possible with this activity.

#94: Boat Parts Relay

Playing Area: Indoors or outdoors

Supplies: One boat per team, cards with the names of the boat parts on them (one set per team)

Skills: Boat nomenclature

Using index cards, write the names of various boat parts on a card, one part per card. Laminate to protect them from getting wet. Make several identical sets of cards, so you can play with a larger group.

Divide the group into teams (teams of three to four people per boat is usually a good number). You will need one boat per team, set far enough apart from each other so players can run around the boats and not collide with the team next to them. Each team gathers around their canoe or kayak, and gets a set of cards, which have the names of the various parts of the boat on them. They may not look at the cards until you say start. At the start, team members look at their cards, and work together to place each card on the corresponding part of the boat. (For example, they will lay the card that reads "Bow deck plate" on the bow deck plate, and so forth.) The first team to correctly place all of their cards is the winner. Be sure to include things like flotation, and things you can't physically see, such as the pivot point. To add extra challenge to the game, throw in some cards with old boating terms, or nomenclature that doesn't apply to that particular kind of boat (they *will* try to place the pirate's gangplank in the boat somewhere).

#95: Fashion Show

Playing Area: Indoors or outdoors

Supplies: Scenario cards, large assortment of clothing that is appropriate and not appropriate for paddling

Skills: Learning about proper clothing for various water and weather conditions

Scenario Cards: Make up a number of paddling scenarios, which you will write on index cards. Each scenario should include information about the weather conditions, water temperature, water conditions, and anything else you think is relevant for the participants to know. (For fun, include a few nonsensical scenarios, such as going to the circus to paddle, which will allow participants to pull the silly clothing items out of the pile.)

Clothing Box: Gather a large assortment of appropriate paddling clothing and gear as well as inappropriate clothing and gear. Be sure to include a few outrageous items, and really mix it up to make this game more fun. Damaged lifejackets are also a good item to include.

Divide the group into three or four teams. Space each team apart from the others. Place the clothing box in the center of the room. Before each round of play, each team selects one of their team members to dress. At the start, one member of the team runs to the front of the room, grabs a scenario card, and takes it back to their team. They then have to grab items from the clothing pile and dress their person appropriately. Once every team is finished, have a fashion show where the team members explain why they picked the clothing they did.

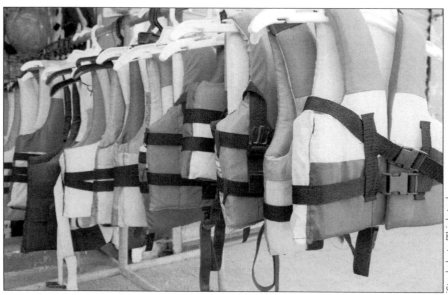

iStockphoto/Thinkstock

#96: Boat Parts Puzzle

Playing Area: Indoors or outdoors
Supplies: Boat parts puzzle (make ahead)
Skills: Boat nomenclature

To Make the Boat Parts Puzzle: Each part of the boat is a separate piece, which the participants will lay in place to "build" the boat. The base piece is the bird's-eye view of the shape of the hull. The rest of the pieces are placed in layers on top of the base. For example, make the following pieces for a canoe: hull (the basic shape of the canoe as the base piece), thwarts (three), seats (bow and stern), gunwales (two: port, starboard), centerline, deck plates (bow and stern), and so forth. To make it more challenging, add more parts, such as painters, battens, amidships, flotation, ribs, and the like.

Make the puzzle large enough so that the pieces aren't miniature and are easy to handle, and so many participants can add parts. Kids will enjoy a giant puzzle; if you can get your hands on a refrigerator box, the large size cardboard makes a great hull base.

#97: Design a Boat

Playing Area: Indoors or outdoors
Supplies: Design cards (make ahead), art supplies (cardboard, tape, scissors, paper, etc.)
Skills: Learning about boat design

This activity is designed to be used in conjunction with curriculum taught on the topic of boat design. Participants play the role of boat designers, and "build" a boat to meet the needs of someone who wants to buy one to be used for a specific purpose.

One at a time, each participant draws a "Boat Wanted" card and then, using the art supplies, designs and constructs a three-dimensional boat that is suitable for the paddling activity listed on the card. After completing their boat construction, participants show their boat, and explain the features and why it's good for the paddling activity listed on the design card.

To Make the "Boat Wanted" Cards: On each index card, write down various different needs that someone wanting to buy a boat would have. For example, "Boat Wanted: Need a canoe that will work well on a big lake that has a lot of large waves and can carry three people easily, plus the dog." or "Boat Wanted: I am buying a new canoe to paddle on a whitewater river. I want something that will maneuver fast." Vary the technical difficulty of the cards to suit the clientele served.

#98: Soap Boats

Playing Area: Indoors or outdoors
Supplies: Bar of Ivory® soap for each person, pocketknives
Skills: Concepts of boat design

This activity is designed to be used in conjunction with curriculum taught on the topic of boat design. Participants get to combine some good old-fashioned camp-craft skills of working with a pen knife and carving with boat design. Before conducting this activity, participants should have training in the safe and proper use of a pocketknife, and be sure to enforce proper knife safety rules during use. Bars of Ivory soap are used for this activity because they are easy to carve, and Ivory soap floats, so you can actually put the boat in a bucket or bathtub afterward and test it out.

After everyone is proficient in pocketknife safety, participants design and carve their canoe or kayak (refer to www.ivory.com/PureFun_IvoryProjects_SoapCarvingTips.htm for carving tips). After everyone completes their boat, have a wee boat show, where each designer explains the features of their boat and what kind of paddling activities it would be suited for. Then, using a large tub or other water-holding implement, test out the boats.

Photo Courtesy of The U.S. Coast Guard

#99: The Clock on the Wall

Playing Area: Indoors or outdoors, with lots of room to spread out
Supplies: Paddles (one per person), masking tape or sidewalk chalk
Skills: Dry-land paddling practice, working on precision paddle placement

This activity teaches precise paddle placement. First, each participant will need to set up their "clock." Participants should space themselves 10 to 12 feet apart from their neighbor. Everyone should be facing the same direction. The center of the clock is where the participant is standing. Have the participant place a small X on the floor with tape or chalk to indicate the center point. From this center point, have each participant take four steps straight forward and mark this spot as "12." Then, again from this center point, have each participant take four steps straight backward and mark this spot as "6." Then, again from this center point, have each participant take four steps right and mark this spot as "3," and do the same thing to the left for "9." This spacing will give you a rough circle for your clock face (add the remaining numbers if desired). If doing this activity on a sandy beach, you can simply "carve" the clock with the paddle.

To conduct the activity, have participants stand in the middle of their clock with a paddle. If practicing canoeing strokes, give direction as if they are bow paddlers or stern paddlers. Then, call out various turning strokes to have the participants practice, such as a forward quarter sweep. As they paddle, have participants pay attention to where their strokes start and stop on the clock. It is often helpful to have everyone paddle in unison and say what they are doing aloud, such as, "The stroke starts at 12 and ends at 3." This activity is also good for enforcing the concepts of rotating the upper body and following the paddle blade with the head, keeping the upper body "in the paddler's box."

#100: Boat Ballet

Playing Area: Indoors or outdoors

Supplies: Canoe paddlers (one per person), source for playing music, CDs, or songs from an MP3 player

Skills: Mentally connecting strokes and maneuvers, communication

For this activity, participants will choreograph a paddling-dance routine for their imaginary tandem canoe to a selected song. The intent is to try to air-paddle coordinated strokes and maneuvers as realistically as possible, in a flowing dance, as if they were really in the boat out on the water. Have each participant grab a buddy as their paddling partner for their imaginary tandem canoe, pick a song, and go. Allow enough time for participants to practice and really get their moves down, and then hold your very own boat ballet.

#101: I Did It My Way

Playing Area: Indoors or outdoors

Supplies: Canoes (at least two, ideally one per team)

Skills: Canoe carrying methods

The object of the activity is for each team to come up with as many different ways to carry a canoe as possible. Once a carry is demonstrated, it cannot be repeated (the same type of carry may be done with a different number of team members, however). For each carry completed, the team gets a point. The team with the most points at the end wins.

Divide your group into even-numbered teams, ideally with no more than six on a team. Explain the task, and give them a few moments to strategize. Select an order, and then start the game. Part of the fun includes creating a little friendly competition between the groups as well. While demonstrating their carry, the team throws down the gauntlet with an, "I carry my boat this a'way. How do you carry yours?" At this point, the other team has to pick up and carry their team's canoe in a different way than what has been already demonstrated. They, too, exchange an, "I carry my boat this a'way How do you carry yours?" and the other team demonstrates another way to carry the boat. This back-and-forth goes on until they exhaust all possible types of carrying.

References

American Camp Association (2006). American Camp Association's *Accreditation Process Guide*. Monterey, CA: Healthy Learning.

American Canoe Association (1996). *Introduction to Paddling: Canoeing Basics for Lakes and Rivers.* Springfield, VA: American Canoe Association/Menasha Ridge Press.

American Red Cross (1981). *Canoeing and Kayaking.* Washington, DC: American Red Cross.

American Red Cross (1998). *Small Craft Safety.* St. Louis, MO: Mosby Lifeline.

American Red Cross (1998). *Basic Water Rescue and Small Craft Safety Instructor's Guide.* St. Louis, MO: Mosby Lifeline.

Escapades!. Lake Mills, WI: Learned Enterprises International.

Kreidler, W. & Furlong, L. (1995). *Adventures in Peacemaking.* Hamilton, MA: Project Adventure, Inc.

Ray, S. (1992). *The Canoe Handbook: Techniques for Mastering the Sport of Canoeing.* Harrisburg, PA: Stackpole Books.

Sobel, J. (1983). *Everybody Wins.* New York: Walker and Company.

U.S. Coast Guard Boating Safety Division. *Lifejacket Wear/Wearing Your Lifejacket.* Retrieved on September 17, 2010, from www.uscgboating.org.

Resources for More Information

American Camp Association
www.acacamps.org
(765) 342-8456

American Canoe Association
www.americancanoe.org
(540) 907-4460

American Red Cross
www.redcross.org
Refer to your local chapter.

American Whitewater Affiliation
www.americanwhitewater.org
(866) BOAT-4-AW

Leave No Trace Center
for Outdoor Ethics
www.lnt.org
(800) 332-4100

National Association of State
Boating Law Administrators
www.nasbla.org
(859) 225-9487

National Safe Boating Council
www.safeboatingcouncil.org
(703) 361-4294

National Water Safety Congress
www.watersafetycongress.com
(440) 209-9805

Project Adventure
www.pa.org
(800) 468-8898

United States Coast Guard Boating
Safety Division
www.uscgboating.org

United States Power Squadrons
www.usps.org
(888) 367-8777

Alphabetical Listing of the 101 Games and Activities

Title	Number	Chapter
… And Then	77	8
Air Paddling	93	10
Aliens, Cows, and Farmers	41	6
Ants on a Log	6	4
Apple, Orange, Banana	66	7
Backwards Ball	88	9
Backwards Bugs	9	4
Balance Buoy	61	7
Barrel Racing	67	7
Batty Baseball	43	6
Blindfold Trust Paddle	26	6
Boat Ballet	100	10
Boat-Over-Boat Relays	15	5
Boat Parts Puzzle	96	10
Boat Parts Relay	94	10
Boat Shapes	87	9
Bow Balloon	78	8
Build-a-Boat Regatta	91	9
Charm School	62	7
Clock on the Wall, The	99	10
Clothespin Tag	28	6
Cow Tipping	17	5
Dead Fish Polo	30	6
Design a Boat	97	10
Dodgeball Tag	50	6
Downriver Racing	71	8
Duck	21	6
Duck, Duck, Goose	29	6
Elbow Tag	44	6
Elevator Up	73	8
Eyes Wide Shut	75	8
Fashion Show	95	10
Ferry-ly We Roll Along	69	7

Title	Number	Chapter
Fish Sticks	82	9
Flash Frozen Fish	84	9
Flippers Up	3	4
Follow the Leader	36	6
Freeze Tag	31	6
Frozen Duck Relay	38	6
Gator Turns	65	7
Gauntlet, The	79	8
Goldilocks and the Three Lifejackets	14	5
Go to Whoa	22	6
Go With the Flow	68	7
Help and Huddle	16	5
Hoop Hurl	52	6
I Did It My Way	101	10
It's an Eddy, Eddie	70	7
Leapfrog	5	4
Lifejacket Fit for a Friend	13	5
Marching Band	34	6
Martian Meteor	83	9
Mirror, Mirror	49	6
Objects Up	81	9
Obstacle Course	35	6
One-of-Each-ie	32	6
Paddle Grip Flip	25	6
Paddle Parts Song, The	92	10
Paddler Party, The	86	9
Pass Tag	40	6
People Paddle	7	4
Pontoon Platoon	57	6
Progression Tag	39	6
Protector Tag	33	6
Push Ball Relay	53	6
Put Down My Coconuts	58	6
Rabbits and Hunters	37	6
Red Light, Green Light	23	6
Rescue Rodeo	20	5
Rock'n'Roll	74	8
Seal Races	2	4
Serpentine	63	7
Sheep and Wolves	76	8

Title	Number	Chapter
Ships to Sea	42	6
Sing Down	10	4
Sky Writing	24	6
Slip'n'Slide	8	4
Slow Motion	1	4
Snakes and Eights	64	7
Soap Boats	98	10
Spin It to Win It	90	9
Spud	56	6
Square Dance	59	6
Stalker	60	6
Star Light, Star Bright	85	9
Steal the Bacon	54	6
Stop, Drop, and Roll	18	5
Strainer Swim	80	8
Synchronized Paddling	27	6
Throw Bag Relay	19	5
Traffic Cop	46	6
Train Track	48	6
Trust Lean	4	4
Turtle Races	11	4
Turtles and Teacups	12	4
Twister Tag	51	6
Upriver Racing	72	8
Vampire Tag	45	6
What's the Time, Mr. Wolf?	55	6
Yo-Yo	47	6
Zigball	89	9

About the Author

Diane Tyrrell has been falling out of boats since the age of 5. Her paddlesports instructional background includes various instructor-level certifications in canoeing and kayaking, from flatwater through whitewater. She currently holds boating certifications at the Instructor and Instructor Trainer levels with the American Canoe Association and the American Red Cross. Additionally, Tyrrell also has an extensive background in lifeguarding, water safety, swimming instruction, and aquatics risk management, and she maintains a number of instructor-level certifications in these areas as well.

Tyrrell has over 30 years experience in the aquatics instructional arena. She has taught canoeing and kayaking activities and instructor-level certification courses for camps, municipalities, universities, parks and recreation programs, and youth organizations, including the Girl Scouts, Boy Scouts, YMCA, 4-H, and Special Olympics.

Tyrrell has contributed content to and been a technical advisor for the American Red Cross *Small Craft Safety* and *Lifeguard Management* training curriculums, as well as provided content for *Camp Waterfront Management* by Cathy Scheder. Additionally, she has had a number of articles published in *Camping Magazine*.

Tyrrell is the director of Camp Motorsport, a race car–driving specialty summer camp for kids ages 9 to 16 located in Virginia. She holds a bachelor's degree in youth agency administration, a bachelor's degree in commercial art, and a Master's degree in education, as well as a professional certification as a Certified Camp Director through the American Camp Association. Tyrrell has over 20 years experience in the camp and youth development field, and is widely respected within the summer camp industry as an expert on aquatics risk management and training and staffing topics, and she has been a speaker at multiple American Camp Association national and regional conferences. Additionally, she is the CEO of Frog Pond Aquatics, which offers aquatics certification and training, aquatics program management consulting, and risk-assessment assistance for program operators, as well as for insurance providers and those in the legal profession.